Praise for *Extraordinary Outcomes*

"Firstenberg and Rubinstein present an excellent, absorbing, and multi-faceted book. It is a deep and wide-ranging guide for thought and action. This book will help leaders guide the organization to identify and concentrate on the major significant factors related to its mission in the face of data overload in a rapidly changing environment."

—**Dan Tolkowsky**
Former Commander of the Israeli Air Force;
Former CEO, Bank Discount Investments

"Iris and Moshe have tied together the latest thinking in business management, behavioral economics, neurology, and psychology into a must-read management strategy treatise. This well-researched and well-written book will help my officers, both ashore and at sea, achieve extraordinary outcomes."

—**Alan B. Buckelew**
Chief Operations Officer, Carnival Corporation

"Iris Firstenberg and Moshe Rubinstein have written a truly remarkable book that is a joy to read. The examples, stories, and illustrations are by themselves a treasure trove of lessons that can guide individuals, teams, organizations, and companies to a happier and more successful future. The authors, however, go much further. Drawing on findings and concepts from decision-making, learning, and brain research, they construct an interpretative framework that provides a guide for achieving the 'extraordinary outcomes' that are the focus of their book."

—**Robert A. Bjork**
Distinguished Research Professor, UCLA
—**Elizabeth L. Bjork**
Professor, UCLA

"Inspirational leadership can be achieved by applying the concepts of this book, an essential guide for today's leader striving to create extraordinary outcomes."

—**Ana Duarte McCarthy**
Chief Diversity Officer, Citi

"Get ready for an entertaining read, practical advice, insights, and leadership lessons that you'll want to put to use immediately!"

—**Sonya Sepahban**
Sr. VP, General Dynamics

"I cannot heap enough praise on *Extraordinary Outcomes*. The concepts are straightforward, intuitive, and when applied—with purpose and deliberate practice—can literally change a culture. I've experienced it firsthand in my organization and witnessed the excitement and commitment from my team. The book will help create a culture of ROI—relentless ongoing improvement—well into the future! The book is awesome! I am having my kids read it and plan to give it out to my team."

—**Katherine Adkins**
VP and General Counsel, Toyota Financial Services

"My team and I were fortunate to experience the content of *Extraordinary Outcomes* when Iris spent a day with us. Iris has mastered the art of educating, inspiring creativity and empowering people to perform beyond even their own expectations. Her riveting stories and practical exercises have helped unite my team and foster a strong sense of purpose. As a result, we are constantly seeing new possibilities, achieving ambitious goals and setting our sights even higher."

—**Christopher Owen**
VP, Integrated Marketing, USAA

"Iris and Moshe have done it again! Their new book is a clear, informative road map to extraordinary outcomes. This gem should be read by people in business, government, and by anyone focused on self-improvement. We are fortunate to have Moshe and Iris tell us their story."

—**Steven Lee Yamshon**
Chief Investment Officer, Stevens First Principles Investment Advisors

"*Extraordinary Outcomes* will engage your heart, your mind, and is a blueprint for excellence at work and at home."

—**Robert Maurer**
Author of *One Small Step Can Change Your Life: The Kaizen Way*

"This remarkably readable treatise guides the reader to become a champion of change and adaptation. Firstenberg and Rubinstein show how inevitable failures and temporary setbacks can become opportunities for cohesion, commitment, and creativity. The authors expertly blend concepts with application to produce extraordinary outcomes."

—**Col (Ret) Mike McKeeman**
The Red Knight, U.S. Army and Raytheon Program
Leadership Deployment Manager

"I had the great fortune to learn from Moshe as a young college student over 25 years ago, and his framework for thinking and problem-solving has impacted my career every step of the way. *Extraordinary Outcomes* captures the brilliant thinking of Moshe and Iris with elegance and simplicity. Moshe has spent a lifetime studying, understanding, and teaching how decisions get made, what leadership is really about, and how to think simply but differently. Iris has added to that with expertise on how the human brain works: Not just what happens, but why. These two perspectives blended together in a way only a father and daughter could achieve provide a compelling formula for achieving extraordinary outcomes."

—John Gavan
President, KPFF Consulting Engineers

"If you are waiting for the world to stabilize, you will be waiting a long time. Constant change and increasing complexity are here to stay, and successful organizations embrace that fact. In this insightful book, Iris Firstenberg and Moshe Rubinstein show how you can create resilient, confident and adaptable teams to achieve extraordinary results in turbulent times."

—Richard F. Ambrose
Executive VP, Lockheed Martin Space Systems

"What is the meaning of life? This question has stymied philosophers for centuries. *Extraordinary Outcomes* gives the reader the answer to a more relevant question, 'What is the meaning of your life?' And this extraordinary book, so aptly titled, goes a step further. It provides pathways to achieve meaning and success in one's own life. It will make a difference in your life."

—Arthur Gilbert
Author, *Under Submission: The First Twenty Years*

"This is an important and thought-provoking book for anyone who aims to promote and better the management of his profession and day-to-day life. The content is conveyed in lucid, vivid language and incorporates relatable and interesting examples and stories. Illustrating applicable methods to define purpose and overcome future uncertainties, the book is brimming with insight, experience, and such fundamental suggestions that the reader will wonder why he had not thought about them before."

—Itzhak Zamir
Former Supreme Court Justice and
Attorney General, State of Israel

Extraordinary
Outcomes

Extraordinary
Outcomes

Shaping an Otherwise Unpredictable Future

IRIS R. FIRSTENBERG

MOSHE F. RUBINSTEIN

WILEY

For general information about our other products and services, please contact our Customer Care Department within the United States at (800) 762-2974, outside the United States at (317) 572-3993 or fax (317) 572-4002.

Wiley publishes in a variety of print and electronic formats and by print-on-demand. Some material included with standard print versions of this book may not be included in e-books or in print-on-demand. If this book refers to media such as a CD or DVD that is not included in the version you purchased, you may download this material at http://booksupport.wiley.com. For more information about Wiley products, visit www.wiley.com.

Library of Congress Cataloging-in-Publication Data:

Firstenberg, Iris R. 1957—
Extraordinary Outcomes: Shaping an Otherwise Unpredictable Future/Iris R. Firstenberg and Moshe F. Rubinstein.
    p. cm.
  Includes index.
ISBN: 978-1-118-93833-1 (cloth); ISBN: 978-1-118-93834-8 (ebk); ISBN: 978-1-118-93835-5 (ebk)
  1. Leadership. 2. Organizational effectiveness. 3. Organizational behavior. 4. Strategic planning. 5. Employee motivation. 6. Uncertainty. I. Rubinstein, Moshe F., II. Title.
    HD57.7.R825 2014
    658.4′092—dc23

                                                                                    2014013527

Printed in the United States of America

10 9 8 7 6 5 4 3 2 1

Contents

1

SKILLS AND TALENT ARE NOT ENOUGH

ENGAGE THE HEAD AND THE HEART

The afternoon knows what the morning never suspected.
—Robert Frost

If you want to make God laugh, tell him your plans.
—Woody Allen

IN AN OCTOBER 2008 BRIEFING BEFORE CONGRESS, a humbled Alan Greenspan, formerly chair of the Federal Reserve Board for almost 19 years, admitted that he had failed to anticipate the ongoing financial collapse, and was in "shocked disbelief" at the way events had unfolded.[1] The world is inherently uncertain, and his inability to foresee the future is only one of endless examples; there are many stories of people and organizations derailed by the emergence of the unexpected. Movie-rental industry leader Blockbuster Entertainment, for example, met its demise when it failed to anticipate the impact that the Internet would have on the way people watch movies. Each of us has our own stories of being blindsided and asking, "How did I not see that coming?"

Conventional ways of thinking and planning fall short in the face of uncertainty, making us vulnerable and ill equipped to respond to the unforeseen. To succeed and thrive in a changing environment, we need strategies that make us more resilient against a shifting future.

In this book we take uncertainty to task, showing that you can conquer it and shape the future to create extraordinary outcomes. You will find an innovative approach to thinking and planning, as well as strategies to navigate uncertainty—to eliminate it where possible, to reduce it where you can, and to be ready to embrace it effectively everywhere else.

Our framework has three components: embracing purpose, engaging people, and expanding the range of possibilities. In the chapters ahead, we weave these components into strategies for thinking and principles for action. Using this framework, you will develop the adaptive capacity to lead both yourself and others into the future.

The ideas we share with you are the result of research in multiple fields and our work with numerous organizations. Our examples reflect a wide spectrum of the human experience and illustrate the broad applicability of our approach to individual, team, and enterprise-wide pursuits. The principles can be applied to your personal as well as your professional life. Along the way you will be introduced to cutting-edge research into how the brain can be harnessed to think more effectively, as well as powerful stories that illustrate how others have successfully created ways to think, plan, and shape their futures.

We start with a story.

Stars and Success

In 1989, a rule change by the International Basketball Federation allowed professional basketball players to compete in the Olympic Games. Fans of the sport in the United States were ecstatic; they felt like they had been handed a permanent ticket to the gold medal. The United States Olympic Committee (USOC) thought so, too. The formula would be simple—recruit top NBA players, send them to the games, and success would be assured. After all, who could hope to compete against the elite of the sport? Uncertainty about who would bring home the gold was over.

The 1992 Olympics were the first games to feel the effect of the rule change. The team roster included Michael Jordan, Magic Johnson, Larry Bird, Charles Barkley, and Scottie Pippin, recognizable names even to people who know almost nothing about the sport. Experts dubbed them the "Dream Team," and many considered this group to be the greatest sports team ever to play together. Although these players had more experience competing against each other than collaborating, the combined force of their talent would make them unbeatable.

The athletes arrived in Barcelona, site of the 1992 games, and after little more than 15 practice sessions together, they won every match. In fact, the games were more like a massacre than a competition. The point spread between the Dream Team and other teams averaged 44 points per game and, for the first time in Olympic history, Team USA did not call for a single time-out. And how did the other teams react? Athletes on the opposing teams were in awe of these guys. In fact, the other players seemed more interested in photo opportunities with Michael Jordan and getting Magic Johnson's autograph than trying to win.

For the USOC, the results validated their definitive formula for success: send in the stars and bring home the gold. And so, four years later, the formula was applied again. NBA players were recruited, and they showed up, won every game, and brought back the gold in 1996. Ditto for 2000. The USA felt invincible.

In 2004, once again NBA players were recruited and sent to the games in Athens, under the assumption that the formula for success was a certainty. To the astonishment of the entire country, Team USA did not win gold. They didn't even win silver. They ended up with the bronze medal . . . and even this was not assured until the final minutes of the game against Lithuania. The team was in shock, the country was in shock, and the USOC was in shock—what had gone wrong?

Reflection

Lack of talent was clearly not the problem. The NBA players on the 2004 Olympic team in 2004—including LeBron James, Dwyane Wade, Lamar Odom, Carmelo Anthony, and Allen Iverson—were athletes at the top of their game and extraordinarily skilled.

Serious soul searching was needed. To help rethink the formula for success, the USOC recruited coach Mike Krzyzewski, the highly successful head of the men's basketball program at Duke University, to help them make sense of the 2004 debacle. Coach K, as he is affectionately known, agreed to analyze the game tapes. Thorough review surfaced amazingly clear signals that had been ignored.

Although the teams from 1992 to 2000 had been undefeated as they played their way to gold, what nobody had paid attention to was that the point spreads were getting smaller. The Dream Team's margins of 44 points per game were closer to 32 points per game in 1996. In 2000 the margins were about 21 points per game, and several of the wins were absolute nail-biters, with Team USA winning some games by only two points. When a match takes place between a strong and a weak contender, the weaker side has much more to learn from the strong team than the other way around. While Team USA basked in the glory of their wins, the teams from competing countries had become relentless in their study and desire to improve.[2]

After analyzing the tapes, Coach K's assessment of what was missing was provocative in its simplicity and its application, both to basketball and, more widely, to all domains of human affairs. He identified two core troubling issues.

Lack of Purpose

Coach K found the first problem to be a lack of team purpose. He vividly explained the problem by saying that each player was playing for his own personal reputation and the name on the back of his jersey; what they needed to play for was the three letters on the front of the jersey, USA. The players needed an emotional connection to a more meaningful purpose than individual glory.

The first challenge, then, would be to engage their heart.

Lack of System

Coach K found the second problem to be a lack of a system. He saw that the players were great but the system was not. The tapes showed that each player was playing his own game. LeBron James was playing the LeBron James game, Dwyane Wade was playing the Dwyane Wade game, Carmelo Anthony was playing the Carmelo Anthony game, and so on. Each player was an exceptional athlete in his own way, but there were as many different games being played as there were players on the court. There was no coordinated, collaborative effort that could be described as the Team USA game. And it wasn't their fault. There was no system in place.

The second challenge, then, would be to create one mind, a mind of Team USA.

To create a path for future success, Coach K accepted the role of head coach for the 2008 Olympic men's basketball team.

We Begin with the End

The athletes on the 2008 USA men's basketball team won the gold medal. But the defining moment came during the medal ceremony, just after the players were awarded their individual medals. In team Olympic sports, each player gets a medal but the coach does not. An unprecedented scene occurred when all the players spontaneously took the medals off their necks and hung them around Coach K's. He stood there, wearing all the medals, surrounded by his team, a testament that they were truly in it together, a team of one heart and one mind.

Coach K repeated his successful program when he coached the 2012 men's basketball team, and he has agreed to coach the team for the 2016 Olympics.

What did Coach K do to shape the success of Team USA? We are going to hit "pause" on the story for now, but don't worry, we will come back to it. In the chapters to come, we will reveal the strategy Coach K used in the context of principles each of us can apply to create extraordinary outcomes.

What Awaits

We hear of the one-shot wonders that are in the right place at the right time and achieve a remarkable result, or the group that sacrifices everything to meet an audacious goal, only to collapse from exhaustion and burnout in the aftermath. There is no surefire guarantee that Team USA will win the gold medal in all future Olympics.

Shaping a rewarding future and achieving extraordinary outcomes does not mean flawless and certain perfection forever. It means that we have a system in place that gives us the optimal framework to think bigger and reach farther, to quickly recover and adapt when plans meet unexpected circumstances, and to perpetually find value as we strive for relentless improvement in pursuit of our goals.

The question we have asked ourselves is:

How can we create extraordinary outcomes in a world of uncertainty?

The story of the 2008 basketball team, and the stories of many other types of teams that we have worked with and studied, have given us insight into the answer to this question. Whether building your personal journey, coaching teams in sports, or leading teams in organizations, the same principles apply. We need to embrace purpose, engage people, and expand our range of possibilities. In the following chapters we describe the principles of the system needed to successfully navigate and shape the future. Along the way we will share lots of stories of individuals and organizations that have created remarkable value, and as we discuss principles, we will also describe in detail how Coach K helped the athletes of Team USA become a team of one heart and one mind.

In Chapter 2, "Connect to a Compelling Purpose," we begin with the importance of purpose in the pursuit of extraordinary outcomes. To be an effective leader of both self and others requires a connection to a purpose that fuels curiosity and helps us navigate into the future, weathering the storms that inevitably arise. We discuss how to find and define a strong and meaningful sense of purpose.

To achieve purpose in a complex world, we can seldom do things alone and even collective efforts are not enough without the right environment. In Chapter 3, "Galvanize Your Team," we describe how to create the environment that builds team alignment for seamless action.

People bring their whole brain to work—both the rational and the emotional. Research in neuroscience has created greater understanding of the profound role emotion plays in human thinking. Positive emotions help to optimize functioning of the rational brain, and in Chapter 4, "Amplify the Positive," we discuss ways to bring out the best in ourselves, our teams, and our organizations to enhance resilience, engagement, and sustainable change.

In Chapter 5, "Conquer Uncertainty," we present a novel way to think about the future, describing ways to eliminate, reduce, and embrace uncertainty as needed. The approach will help you see more possibilities, become more agile and adaptive, and create strategic advantage in the pursuit of purpose.

Chapter 6, "Acknowledge, Learn, Correct," teaches how to turn failure into learning opportunities for improvement. We will share the provocative strategies experts use to hone their skills in order to excel. You will also learn how people and organizations can recover more quickly from setbacks, and how you can motivate yourself and others when challenges arise.

In Chapter 7, "Shape Your Future," we conclude with a story to inspire you on your journey to conquer uncertainty and create extra-ordinary outcomes.

2

CONNECT TO A COMPELLING PURPOSE

FUEL CURIOSITY AND IGNITE FUTURE-FOCUSED THINKING

The Purpose of Purpose

In Greek mythology, the deceitful King Sisyphus is doomed to spend eternity pushing a large boulder up a steep mountain, only to have it roll back down just before it reaches the top, forcing him to start over again. In another Greek myth, Penelope, wife of the absent Odysseus, sits all day at her loom, painstakingly weaving a burial shroud, only to unravel it each night and start again the next morning.

The repetitive work of Sisyphus is frustrating and meaningless, and is designed as punishment, to torture its victim. But what about Penelope's? She has willingly chosen a task that on the surface appears to be no different from the burden of Sisyphus—doing, undoing, and redoing work. However, her work has great meaning. Her husband has not returned from war but she believes he is still alive. To ward off suitors while she waits for his return, she agrees to choose one of them as a new husband, but only when she finishes weaving the shroud on her loom. To buy time, she gladly commits to the repetitive job because it holds purpose. Even mundane activity can become meaningful when embedded in the richer context of purpose.

Purpose is the magnetic pull that draws us into the future, injecting us with resilience to overcome stumbles and reinterpret tedious tasks along the way. Purpose acts as a filter, helping us determine what we have to pay attention to, and what we can safely ignore. Purpose creates focus and fuels our curiosity, helping us more quickly identify uncertainties that are unfolding so that we can more quickly adapt. Imagine an airplane on the runway at JFK. The pilot's purpose is to safely deliver passengers to a particular destination. He does not take off unless he knows where he is heading. Whatever turbulence there might be along the way to force the plane off course, the pull of the destination helps the pilot navigate the plane back on track. Without a clear destination, any storm the plane encounters becomes the force that controls it, dictating the direction it will go. Without purpose, we are like the plane without a destination; the turmoil of uncertainty overpowers and controls us. With a clear and compelling purpose, we prevail despite unfolding turbulence; we adapt, improvise, and adjust our course of action.

Purpose and Meaning

Victor Frankl, an Austrian psychiatrist, developed a theory about the importance of purpose while he was held captive in a Nazi concentration camp.[1] He observed that physically stronger people, under the most horrific and inhumane of conditions, could die before those who were weaker—prompting him to wonder what could be a factor in survival beyond physical strength. Frankl isolated the critical difference: people who had a purpose, a reason to go on living, found the inner strength to prevail and survive; those who had lost their purpose would soon succumb and die. In his book *Man's Search for Meaning*, he explains that pursuit of meaningful purpose is more crucial as a path to happiness in our lives than the pursuit of pleasure. We want to feel that our lives have meaning and that we are engaged in endeavors that matter. With a clear sense of purpose the narrative of our life has coherence, and we have greater resilience and ability to persevere despite setbacks that inevitably unfold. Those who spend their lives in the pursuit of fleeting pleasures often feel like Sisyphus—no matter how much they try, it's never enough to fill the void they sense within, and the slightest disappointments can be derailing.

Work with Purpose

In 1942 the world was engulfed in war. It was believed that Nazi Germany was moving swiftly to develop the atomic bomb. Before war had broken out, Niels Bohr, Albert Einstein, Leo Szilard, and other leaders in the scientific community of the free world had been alarmed that the United States was not responding urgently enough to counter the efforts of the Nazis. When President Roosevelt finally realized just how imminent the threat was, he responded by launching the Manhattan Project. For this top-secret mission, the best brains in science secretly gathered in Los Alamos, New Mexico. Their goal would be to beat Nazi Germany in unlocking the power of the nucleus and be first to build the atomic bomb.

At Los Alamos, Richard Feynman, only 24 years old, was appointed to a role we would today call CIO (chief information officer). He would lead a group of top math and science students from the best universities to serve as human computers; they would do all the detailed calculations to provide the data needed by the physicists. They used only slide rules and primitive calculators, so you can imagine how tedious, tiring, and boring the long hours of cranking out numbers quickly became for these students. They were unaware of the purpose of the mission, and the results reflected just how uninspired they were. The accuracy of their work left a lot to be desired, and their lagging pace frustrated the scientists as well.

Feynman realized that his team was not living up to its potential. It dawned on him that they were unmotivated because they had no clue what they were working on—what the purpose of the work was. He met with Robert Oppenheimer, one of the project leaders, and shared his frustration. They petitioned for and received a clearance from the highest level of government to share the purpose of the project with these young students. After they were sworn to secrecy, the purpose of the project was revealed to them. Imagine how these students felt when they were told that the project for which they had been recruited was so awesome, important, and secret that the fate of the entire free world might depend on their work, their dedication, and their utmost discretion.

Feynman found that in the following days the accuracy, pace, and amount of work produced by the students increased dramatically. They no longer thought of the work as a burden to bear, but as a responsibility to fulfill as their contribution to the noble purpose of saving the free world.[2]

Team USA Finds Its Purpose

Coach K also understood that his players needed a grand purpose to galvanize their efforts, a purpose that was compelling and meaningful. A terrific opportunity to give voice to this purpose and engage their hearts occurred on a promotional trip that the team took to New York City in June of 2008.

As part of the itinerary, they sailed to Ellis Island for a team photo in front of the Statue of Liberty. Aboard the tour boat, Coach K spoke movingly to the team about his grandfather, who had emigrated from Poland and who undoubtedly had made great sacrifices to create a life for his family in the land of opportunity. Now, here he was, just two generations later, with the opportunity to coach the team representing that American dream. He reminded each one of them that they, too, had ancestors who had struggled in this country—ancestors who worked long and hard, fueled by their hopes for the future, to make it possible for their children and grandchildren to have the incredible opportunities they were now living.[3]

Coach K suggested that each of their ancestors deserved to be recognized. He proposed that while singing the national anthem at the start of each game, they should each hold their hand over their heart, look at the flag, think about their ancestor, and then get on the court and play basketball to honor that person. The players were visibly moved.

To broaden and deepen their connection to a purpose larger than themselves, Coach K also introduced the players to three wounded soldiers who had returned home from war. Each of these soldiers had put the needs of others above their own, and even now, despite their intense injuries, they insisted on continuing their careers in the military to serve their country. The soldiers were invited to meet the team at one of its early practice sessions, and each one told his story, about selfless service and why he wanted to continue to serve. The colonel who accompanied the visit gave each player a small flag, the same flag worn by every soldier serving abroad. He asked them to wear the flags on their uniforms, as a reminder that they, too, were representing the values of their country. The tears in the eyes of the players convinced Coach K that they now had a shared sense of their purpose.[4]

In the rest of this chapter, we will discuss three levels of purpose; the organization, the team, and the individual. We will discuss why purpose matters at the level of an organization, how a team articulates the meaning of their work, and what each individual can do to identify their personal sense of purpose.

Purpose in an Organization

Just as Coach K helped Team USA identify a compelling shared purpose, it is equally important to articulate in the corporate setting.

People in organizations are caught up in the busy-ness of business, often juggling several projects at the same time. While all assignments require a baseline of effort, certain projects get our discretionary effort—the attention that is voluntary and goes well beyond the minimum required. To which projects do we dedicate ourselves more wholly? To those projects that are meaningful, to those that reward us intrinsically with a sense of purpose, the projects we believe will make a difference. The role of a leader, then, is to involve a team in a conversation about *why* the work matters, before focusing on *what* tasks need to be done.

Leaders Inspire with Purpose

The most effective leaders have rallied people to action by articulating a noble purpose that rouses emotions. A noble purpose that grabs the heart is what fuels hope. It gives us the courage and fortitude to take a stand even when the present appears bleak. Abraham Lincoln is remembered for the Gettysburg Address, a speech that is only 10 sentences long, which took Lincoln less than three minutes to deliver. It still stirs people today, because the speech is about purpose— invoking the principle of human equality spelled out in the Declaration of Independence, and exhorting citizens to ensure that "government of the people, by the people, for the people, shall not perish from the earth." John F. Kennedy mobilized a generation by urging them to "ask not what your country can do for you, but what you can do for your country." From this purpose emerged the Peace Corps and (even years later), AmeriCorps, to name but two of the socially redeeming projects it inspired. Kennedy then challenged the nation to reach for the stars when in 1961 he declared that the nation would commit to the goal, "before this decade is out, of landing a man on the moon and returning him safely to the earth." Thousands of students flocked to schools of science and engineering to be part of the dream. Years later, Barack Obama moved people to vote by firing their imaginations with his simple "Yes, we can."

You don't have to be a historical giant to do what these famous leaders have done. The common thread in these inspiring calls for action is their brevity, simplicity, and focus on value. A friend of ours, a project manager at a large network communications company, was charged with designing the software for the home screen of a new smartphone. His tech-savvy team was uninspired; for them it was just another software project. He realized that he had to shift their frame of mind and mobilize them around the purpose of their work. "We're not just writing software code," he told them. "Every one of us knows someone who is intimidated by technology. Our task is to make it more accessible. Our work touches people and will give everyone an equal chance to connect." This shift in perspective galvanized the team and they came up with ideas that exceeded all expectations. He was amazed at the power of purpose.

Although the popular adage tells us that "a picture is worth a thousand words," we would argue that "a word, properly placed, can be worth millions of pictures." A statement of purpose that engages the heart can create expansive pictures of possibilities in the millions of minds that resonate with the message. Just as social leaders create great change by first engaging emotions, so must leaders of organizations inspire people to invent the future by engaging both the head and the heart.

Crafting a Statement of Purpose

Articulating purpose is an art, because in a few short words, it must be compelling and inspiring, give people hope, and stimulate ideas for expanding the scope of possibility. For example, in the late 1980s, President Ronald Reagan sensed that Soviet general secretary Mikhail Gorbachev might be open to strengthening ties with the West. Standing next to the Berlin Wall, Reagan intended his challenge— "Mr. Gorbachev, tear down this wall"—to mean that the concrete wall literally should be dismantled, but more broadly he was asking the Soviets to show that they were serious about partnering for peace. His purpose, using the vivid imagery of tearing down a wall, was instantly and unambiguously understood.

Unfortunately, for many organizations the purported purpose is so vague that it either fails to generate any innovative thought for action, or is so mundane that it fails to inspire. "To be the world's best in our industry" exemplifies the type of vague, self-centered statement that fails to generate a call for action. What constitutes best? Best at what? And why does it matter? Barbara Waugh, a former director at Hewlett-Packard, relays in her book, *The Soul in the Computer*,[5] the crisis of purpose when the company decided to focus its efforts on becoming "the world's best industrial research lab." She bemoans this purpose as too narrow, too inwardly focused. It asked people in the company to think about how to improve the organization, but this dream was just not big enough. Waugh challenged the company to think outward rather than focusing inward, asking not how HP could be "the best industrial research lab *in* the world," but instead "the best industrial research lab *for* the world." By changing just one word, the purpose became expansive, noble, compelling, and contagious. Ideas for contributions to medicine, education, and the environment surged; people became passionate about their work and the contributions they could make toward the purpose.

Statements of purpose that speak to profits or shareholder value also fail to inspire; they don't appeal to our desire to engage in work that is noble, meaningful, and connected to something that transcends ourselves. Profits and shareholder value are outcomes that will ensue if we create something of value; they are not something that can sustainably be pursued in a vacuum of purpose.

Team Purpose

Conversations about purpose do not need to wait for an all-hands, authorized company retreat. Every team can begin today to ask itself, "What is our purpose?" The answer should include not just what you do, but why what you do matters. It can be extremely enlightening to have each team member answer this question individually, by writing it down in a few sentences. If it makes people more comfortable, it can be done anonymously on sticky notes, and then all the statements can be collected on a wall with an opportunity for everyone to look them over. It can be eye opening to see how different the perceptions of colleagues can be. If we don't have this conversation, we might assume that we have a shared team purpose, unaware of the uncertainty that perhaps we do not. Teams that engage in this conversation and emerge with a sense of purpose that resonates with everyone find that they approach their work with renewed vigor, a sense of urgency, and increased creativity.

A powerful example of a conversation about purpose took place with the janitors of a large pharmaceutical company. The leader of the maintenance department had just taken over from her predecessor and was grasping for a way to motivate the team to improve their work ethic. The workers were apathetic and their efforts were sloppy; prior attempts to reward or punish behavior had not resulted in any sustained change. The new leader of the team decided to engage them in a conversation about purpose.

Inviting them into the large conference room, she began by asking questions about their relationship to certain diseases. When it was clear that several of them had family and friends with the diseases she was naming, she said, "You know, the purpose of this organization is to find cures and improve the quality of life for people with those diseases." To her astonishment, there were people in the room who had no idea that this is what the company did. They only knew that they came to work at night to empty trash cans, clean restrooms, and tidy up offices and labs. She realized that sharing this grand purpose of the organization was only part of the missing message. It was not enough to know that the organization did meaningful work; each one of the workers wanted to know why his or her specific efforts added value.

So she continued, "When the scientists come to work in the morning, they are conducting experiments, looking for cures to save lives and improve the quality of life for people with these diseases. If there is dust, or contaminated glass, or missing papers, these problems can potentially compromise the experiments. If we don't do our job, they can't do their job, and cures will not be found. We are part of the team that is going to save the lives of these patients." The change in energy in the room was palpable. People bombarded her with questions and she noticed that they sat up straighter. This was the conversation that turned the team around. She now gets them together once a quarter to revisit the purpose, to reinforce the message that their work matters.

Finding Nobility of Purpose

A TV executive attending one of our classes felt challenged to find the purpose that would motivate his team. He said, "It's pretty easy to see the compelling purpose when you're saving lives. I work for a TV network, and our job is to broadcast garbage. How am I supposed to inspire my team with that?" The other class participants were stunned and there was a moment of complete silence in the room.

Out of this silence, one student stood up and said, "How can you say that? Do you know how important your shows are to me and my family?" He described his elderly, disabled parents, who were living in a full-care facility. With limited mobility, their only entertainment was television and they looked forward each evening to their favorite shows. Most importantly, they had started to watch the same shows as their grandchildren, so that during Sunday family visits they would have something in common to share with the kids. Another class member told him that her young sons found comfort in a particular show that they loved watching with their dad, who was now deployed by the military thousands of miles from home. When they watched the show they would giggle about how much Dad loved a funny character, and it made them feel closer to their absent father.

From these stories, it became clear to the TV executive that purpose must be defined with the end user in mind, through the value that they perceive. Often we don't understand the users' perception until we either live in their world or engage them in a conversation about purpose. Purpose is not in what you do, but rather in the value you create. This TV executive would now be able to approach his work with a sense of purpose that until now had eluded him.

Tap into Uniqueness

A team leader at a top IT firm shared her experience after having the conversation about purpose with her team. She recognized that not only is team purpose important, but that each member should feel that their personal contribution is relevant and meaningful to the team purpose. She asked them, in addition to the responsibilities they each shouldered as part of their job description, "How would you like to uniquely contribute to this purpose? Is there anything you would like to bring to the project that would help us as a team?" She was amazed at the ideas they offered, and in the process learned a lot about each person beyond his or her job role. She credits much of the innovative approach her team now uses simply to having asked this question.

Southwest Airlines states their purpose as "connecting people to what's important in their lives through friendly, reliable, and low-cost air travel." Any employee at any level is welcome to suggest and is empowered to implement new ideas that help fulfill the purpose. In one instance, a passenger could not find his wallet, and the captain overheard him tell the flight attendant that he thought he might have left it in the restaurant of the departure airport. The captain immediately called the airport with his personal phone, located the wallet, and gave the passenger $40 of his own money to help him when he landed.[6]

In an environment where purpose is clear, and people have the freedom to contribute in ways that both support the purpose and allow them the opportunity to shine, extraordinary outcomes accrue. A leader should take every opportunity to give people a chance to bring their best self to work, to grow, and to become what they can be.

Objectives, Goals, Targets

If you don't know where you are going, any road will take you there.
—Attributed to Lewis Carroll

People use a variety of words to describe a reason to take action. *Objective, goal, target*—these give aim to specific local actions. Purpose, however, determines whether the objectives, goals, or targets are relevant. It provides the answer to why particular objectives, goals, or targets are worth pursuing; they are relevant when they are milestones along the trajectory of purpose. The statement of purpose must therefore be simple enough that it provides easily understood boundaries within which such judgments can be made, and compelling enough that it sparks the imagination to create greater objectives, goals, or targets. One of the objectives may include profit, in order to keep the pursuit of purpose sustainable. Profit alone, however, is not a purpose.

Individual Purpose

How I thought it worked was, if you were great, like Martin Luther King, Jr., you had a dream. Since I wasn't great, I figured I had no dream and the best I could do was follow someone else's. Now I believe it works like this: It's having the dream that makes you great. It's the dream that produces the greatness.[7]
—Barbara Waugh

Finding Your Own Purpose

Henry David Thoreau poignantly observed that "most men lead lives of quiet desperation and go to the grave with the song still in them." Many of us struggle to figure out what our song—or purpose—is. We only know that we are vaguely dissatisfied, perhaps have no real idea what to do with ourselves, and imagine that people like Martin Luther King, Jr., or others we know with a strong sense of personal purpose, are profoundly and substantively different from ourselves. We are plagued with doubt, anxiety, and confusion, and compare ourselves disparagingly with our friends who knew from the age of 10 what they wanted to do with their lives. Many think that their only recourse is to try to create *work–life balance*. The implication is that work and life are on the seesaw of a zero-sum war; more work implies less life. This is the mindset of a pie that has a limited size, and the more of the pie that is dedicated to work, the less of the pie can be dedicated to life. Imagine if instead you could attain *work–life integration*, in which the size of the pie grows as your sense of purpose intensifies.

Question Your Wants versus Your Cans

Your personal purpose is not defined by your current skills, by what you think you are good at doing, or what you think (or have been told) you should be doing. When you think about your purpose, considering what you *can* do does not elicit the energy and passion that comes from thinking about what you *want* to do. Why should you initially ignore the *can*? Because when you know your unique purpose, you will want to get better and better at doing what it takes to achieve it, and so you will seek and relish opportunities to develop the skills necessary to succeed. Or you will seek ways to make your weaknesses irrelevant, which we will explore in greater detail in Chapter 5 when we discuss options for partnering with others. What you think you *can* do limits the possibilities you consider; thinking about what you *want* to do taps into your passions and thus helps you to identify your purpose. Too many people settle for an unsatisfying job, or an uninspiring career, instead of finding their calling. When we find our purpose, we may even view our current job in a different light that gives it new significance. Part of our journey is to find our unique purpose, and then act on it, to become happy with our lives in a way that is meaningful.

So what is it that makes work meaningful? College students often answer that it should be visionary, or it has to benefit humanity in some big and impactful way, or it has to be perceived as successful. What then would we say about the young man who thinks about cars all day, dreams about them at night, and spends every free hour fixing dilapidated cars? When he brings an old car back to life he feels exactly what is meant by meaningful work. Work is meaningful when you find an emotional connection with something that is right for you.

One of the profound roles of leadership is to help people tap into their passions and discover the meaning in what they do.

Challenge Your Elephant Beliefs

If you are still trying to figure out your purpose, here is a story about the training of a circus elephant that might help you identify what is stopping you. Before the elephant is brought into the big tent to perform, he must wait in the staging area until the other acts are over. Imagine he is kept in place by a rope tied around his neck that is tethered to a stake in the ground. However, relative to the size of the elephant, the rope looks like dental floss and the stake in the ground is not very strong, either. Nevertheless, the elephant does not challenge the rope. Why? When the elephant was young and small, he was repeatedly brought to the same type of staging area and the rope was put around his neck. At that stage of his life, he tried to fight the rope, to get loose and move around, but eventually learned that the rope was stronger than he was. So he stopped trying. Years have gone by, and the elephant is stronger than the rope, but the only one who does not know it is the elephant. He still believes that the rope is stronger than he is, so he doesn't even try.

We all have our elephant ropes. These are beliefs we have about ourselves that we have internalized over time, usually imprinted during our childhood and adolescence, and that we never stop to question. Some of these beliefs might be truths that were appropriate earlier in our lives but are no longer relevant. For example, a participant in one of our executive programs had wanted to run for public office, but was supporting two young children and struggling to make ends meet, so she abandoned the dream and, as time went on, she forgot about it. In our session, she realized that circumstances had changed, her children were now older, and she could revive the dream. Kids are often asked, "What do you want to be when you grow up?" but this mother needed to ask, "What do I want to be when my kids grow up?"

Other beliefs might be messages that we got from people important in our childhoods that we internalized because of the messenger, not because we particularly agreed with the message. Think of people who were important to you as you were growing up and what they wanted you to do with your life. Dad would be so proud if you went to his alma mater! Mom thinks women should not travel alone. Uncle Bob refuses to talk to his son because he lives on a commune and Dad supports Uncle Bob's decision. And on it goes, messages both direct and indirect, about what you should or should not do. Is there any message that says, "Go out and fulfill your unique destiny!"? If you are like most people, this was not one of the messages you heard growing up—which means you may have to start saying it to yourself.[8]

Purpose Has No Age Limit

A three-year-old child, the youngest of nine in his family, was hospitalized with a very serious illness. It was not clear that he would survive. At home, each child in the family had specific responsibilities, and this little boy's chore had been to keep the stairs clear of clutter. Visiting her son in the hospital, the mom shared with him that without him at home, the stairs were becoming almost impassable. This conversation perceptibly changed his attitude; he became determined to get better, telling the nurses that he had an important job to do. When a person, even a young child, feels needed, they can get a new lease on life, moved by the meaningful purpose to serve others. It is not unreasonable to say that people who are *needed by people* are the luckiest people in the world.

Expand Your Universe to Find Purpose

When Moshe was nine years old, his parents hired an engineer to design what would become their house. Moshe was mesmerized by the engineer and his blueprints and started drawing designs of his own, pretending that he was an engineer. His interest grew and he told everyone that he wanted to be an engineer when he grew up. In college he earned a BS in engineering and applied science and got his first job with a structural design company. For the first few months the work was novel and exciting. All that changed on the day the chief engineer asked him to assist with plans for an underground garage that would be constructed underneath an existing 12-story building. Moshe was honored to be chosen, and quickly went off to retrieve the original drawings from the city archives. He returned with the drawings and jumped right into the work; he was so excited that he lost track of time and worked well into the evening.

After almost everyone had left for the day, one of the older engineers stopped by to see what he was doing. Moshe proudly showed him the preliminary work he had started on the blueprints for the garage and told him, "By the way, the original drawings of the building are amazing! They were done in India ink, and the lettering looks like calligraphy! Here, I'll show you!"

He pulled out the originals, and the older engineer looked startled as he pointed to a box in the lower right corner with the names of the architect and engineers of the original project inscribed along with the date. Visibly moved, he said, "Look! That's my name! I was the engineer on this building!"

In that moment, Moshe's excitement turned to horror. The date on the plans was the year he was born. All he could think was, "This guy was drawing plans more than twenty years ago and he is still doing exactly the same thing now. Am I going to be stuck doing this for the rest of my life?" Moshe's encounter with the older engineer was a defining moment.

On the drive home, he realized that he needed to rethink his future. He still loved engineering, but dreaded the idea of spending his life on tasks that would become routine. Over the next few weeks Moshe began to explore ways to expand the universe of possibilities. Within six months he decided to quit his job and go back to school for graduate degrees in broader fields within engineering and applied science.

Now, imagine if Moshe could have explored his interest in structural engineering as a high school student, shadowing an engineer at work or serving as an intern. Exposure to the real world of working as an engineer might have helped him make a more informed choice before deciding to spend four years studying structural engineering. How many people choose to study a field for all the wrong reasons, and only when they graduate and start to work do they realize the mistake they made? Moshe's defining moment, and the self-reflection that followed, helped him change direction; while in graduate school he realized he had a passion for teaching, research, and mentoring, and he became a professor of engineering and management.

Maybe right now you have a job but feel stuck, and you fantasize about work that will be meaningful and fulfilling. It's tough to find your purpose by sitting at home or limiting your view to whatever is right in front of you. If you haven't found your calling in your current universe of experiences, it's time to expand your universe. Explore and experience! There are terrific opportunities to learn about new possibilities. For example, there are ways to sample alternative careers by shadowing other people. For some the experience turns out to be a reality check; for others it is the trigger that initiates a life change, either a career tweak or a career switch. In all cases, it informs and helps determine whether a particular direction feels right to pursue further. At the very least, seize every opportunity to explore something about a field you know nothing about. Talk to people, search the Internet, read magazines in areas outside your field of knowledge, and expand the universe of possibilities. It's never too late to find purpose.

Purpose, Happiness, and Well-Being

The field of Positive Psychology, pioneered by Martin Seligman, investigates happiness and well-being. There are three routes people take with the purpose of increasing life satisfaction, and combining them leads to the greatest overall sense of well-being. Seligman identifies the three paths as "the pleasant life, the good life, and the meaningful life."

The pleasant life centers on having things. People who engage in retail therapy believe that they can buy enough stuff to make themselves permanently happy. Free coffee at work and getting a bigger office add to the pleasant life. However, the glow quickly fades from whatever is new and we soon need another novel fix. Seligman finds that most people think about the pleasant life when they consider whether they are happy from moment to moment. Focusing only on individual moments leaves people with what Seligman calls "fidgeting until death" syndrome.

The good life revolves around activities: engaging in a hobby, travel, or socializing. We use our unique strengths or interests to enhance our lives. It might include training for and running a marathon, visiting the Seven Wonders of the World, reading interesting books, or working on a challenging project. More durable than the pleasant life, it still leaves us yearning for something more, maybe asking, "Is this all there is?"

The meaningful life creates the sense of well-being that Seligman defines as imperative for happiness. For example, finding a sense of belonging and commitment to a project, idea, or cause, or making a difference for a better world, creates value for something larger than ourselves and enriches our lives as well. By pursuing a meaningful life Seligman does not argue that we will be permanently happy in the giddy, smiley-face, perennially cheerful, and high-spirited definition of the word. To the contrary, pursuing a noble purpose can be fraught with obstacles and frustrating setbacks that must be overcome. Seligman defines true happiness as satisfaction and fulfillment that continue even in the face of difficulty; indeed, there is great satisfaction in finding creative ways to achieve a purpose that is not within easy reach.

The work environment conducive to extraordinary outcomes integrates all three paths to happiness, and people who integrate all three paths to happiness have the greatest overall satisfaction with their lives.[9]

Evolution of Purpose

There comes a time when a purpose may have to be redefined, either because it has been achieved or because it is no longer relevant. Nelson Mandela achieved his purpose of ending apartheid, and then had to ask, "And now what?" John F. Kennedy gave the nation a noble purpose, to put a man on the moon, but that, too, was achieved, and NASA had to ask, "And now what?"

The Canadian town of Chemainus on the east coast of Vancouver Island faced a crisis of purpose in the early 1980s. Founded as a logging town in 1858, the economy was reliant on a single major employer, which can leave a community vulnerable to increased uncertainty. Indeed, when economics dictated closing of the lumber mill, Chemainus faced possible extinction. It would not have been the first community to turn into a ghost town. But the mayor, Graham Bruce, was open to possibilities and seized the opportunity to breathe new purpose into the community. With the public support of residents (affectionately known as Chemaniacs), the town offered the outer walls of its buildings to artists, to cover with murals. Today Chemainus is famous for its outdoor gallery; the 42 murals covering several blocks of the main part of town have spawned a tourist industry that includes over 300 businesses that support the influx of visitors.

Continuous Evolution of Purpose

Companies can also face the "And now what?" question, when the customer no longer finds value in their purpose. Companies that adapt to changing customer needs continue to thrive. Nokia evolved from a paper mill into a telecommunications company, IBM moved from machines to business solutions, and GE has been on the *Fortune* 100 list for over 100 years because it works hard to make its own products obsolete before the competition does it to them. They all think about the value they provide the customer as integral to their purpose for existence.

The companies that do not survive are those that ignore the unfolding future. Anchored to the past, holding on to products or services that brought them great success in an environment that no longer works, they continue to believe that they are relevant, contrary to all the current cues. Blockbuster, for example, continued to believe customers wanted to rent movies from a brick-and-mortar business long after Netflix was proving otherwise. Companies on the *Fortune* 100 list often disappear for the same reason. They are unable to adapt when their original purpose for existence becomes irrelevant. This means we must remain vigilant, questioning our assumptions about relevance, and monitoring the unfolding future for cues that a renewal of purpose may be required.

Vigilance to Redefine Purpose

Questioning purpose and understanding the perception of the customer is what saved a bicycle company trying to sell motorized bikes in India at the end of World War II. With the exception of consistent orders from one part of the country, sales were lackluster. However, as Peter

Drucker tells the story, within a few months, orders from the successful region began to change in an odd way. Customers started requesting that the company sell them just the motor, without the bicycle. At first, the owners balked; after all, they were a bicycle company that happened to also sell motorized bicycles, not a company that sold motors. But one of the owners was curious, and decided to travel to the area to see why people wanted the motors. It turned out that some very creative farmers had found a way to use the motors for field irrigation, upgrading their hand-operated water pumps into motorized water pumps. The company reevaluated its purpose and transformed itself into one of the largest suppliers of motorized water pumps in Southeast Asia.[10]

Define Purpose

As we have shown, a compelling statement of purpose inspires people to focus on value, engages the heart towards work that matters, and stimulates ideas for greater possibilities. We encourage you to use the methods we have described to craft a statement of purpose for yourself, for your team, and the enterprise as a whole. We suggest that you revisit this periodically, perhaps annually, adding and modifying as the future unfolds and your sense of purpose evolves.

■ ■ ■

Working to realize purpose and achieving extraordinary outcomes is rarely a solitary pursuit. In most cases, we need the support and collaboration of others. We each have multiple teams in our lives; for example, colleagues at work, family members at home, social groups, and many others. The tools for effective collaboration can be applied to any of the communities in our network, and in the next chapter we look at principles for galvanizing a team.

3

GALVANIZE YOUR TEAM

Forge Tightly Aligned Teams Poised for Seamless Action

IN A WORLD OF INCREASING COMPLEXITY, we seldom achieve greatness alone. Just about everything we do depends on engaging other people. In this chapter, we look at factors that help deepen our connection with others to pursue purpose.

The Team as Organism

Imagine that your right leg is trying to walk while your left leg is trying to run. The organism we call *YOU* is going to fall flat on your face. Only when all your parts organize to work in unison, with a coordinated effort, can you successfully navigate in the world. You are a living, breathing organism with lots of individual parts—kidneys, shoulders, intestines, eyeballs—and all your limbs and organs have to collaborate and coordinate their efforts for the great purpose of keeping you alive.

A team is also an organism, and the parts, in this case the individual members of the team, have to be organized for success. The parts that make up the team are people who have to collaborate and coordinate their efforts, and it takes a system to create a dynamic, adaptive organism that we can call a great team.

For instance, when the NBA athletes met with Coach K to start their training for the 2008 Olympic Games, they were not yet a team. They were a collection of players with outstanding skills, but they had no system in place to organize for success.

Forging a Team Identity

To create this system, Coach K called a meeting with the athletes. The purpose of the meeting was to forge a team identity that would define how they worked together. He explained that together they would create a set of principles that all of them would commit to uphold.

These principles, or "standards" as he called them, would define what it meant to be the 2008 Team USA. The team would be able to look at the list and say, "That's who we are. We don't just show up; these standards define HOW we show up."[1]

Coach K made it clear that standards are not rules. An example of a rule might be that all players have to be in their rooms with lights out by 9:00 PM. Rules can be insulting or even stupid (and people either follow them or break them), but standards inspire us to be our best. Standards define what we expect of ourselves and each other, no matter the circumstances, even when the going gets tough. Standards are the stabilizing anchors in a world of turbulence and uncertainty.

The conversation became very personal and intimate as the players generated standards and added them to the list. Many of the principles were tied to unselfish and committed behavior, with a collective responsibility to each other. "Trust" and "Communication" were two standards that Coach K asked to include on the list. One of the players said that "Being on Time" is a sign of respect for teammates and that it should be a standard. LeBron James proposed the standard of "No Excuses." They could not blame jet lag, the crowd, the referees, or any other outside factor for failing to live up to their standards. "No Excuses" became the standard at the top of their list.

The team eventually developed 15 standards that included:

No excuses

When we communicate we look each other in the eye

We tell each other the truth

We respect each other and our opponents

We win together and lose together

We give aid to a teammate

We are always on time

Our value is not measured in playing time

We represent the USA at all times

This is fun!

Building Your Team Standards

Most large organizations today have a list of core values. Once the list is generated, the company expects all employees to act in accordance with the values. It's a stretch and a leap, however, between values in the abstract and behavior in the real world. Values that are printed on posters are not enough to motivate behaviors, and often the values are what we say we want but not what we actually experience inside the organization. These core values nevertheless can serve as an excellent platform from which to launch a team conversation about standards. There are universal values that are fundamental to great teams, but as Coach K understood, to own the values and commit to them, every team has to develop the standards that define how members want to collaborate with each other to actually enact the values.

Universal Values to Establish Standards

Universal values we've identified are *trust, respect, integrity, empathy, inclusion,* and *communication.* These values are fundamental for creating a team of one mind that is focused on purpose and equipped to achieve extraordinary outcomes. We look at each in detail; why they matter, what happens when they are ignored, and how to build them into team standards.

Trust

Trust is so essential in all aspects of human interaction that it must be developed and cultivated on an ongoing basis. Trust is the binding force that makes it possible for people working together to achieve extraordinary outcomes.

Intent Is Not Enough

In November 2004, a nurse at a Los Angeles hospital noticed an odd wire dangling from the clock in the break room. When she inspected it more closely, she discovered a hidden camera. Within minutes she alerted all the other nurses in her department, and they quickly found a total of 16 hidden cameras placed in lounges, a conference room, and other areas of their unit. Outraged, they charged into the offices of hospital administrative staff and demanded an explanation. Hospital officials were surprised at the strong reaction, and told them that they had installed the cameras as part of an effort to reduce petty theft. In no way were they accusing the nurses of these thefts, they said, and they had intended to notify people about the cameras, but had not yet done so. They said that the cameras had not yet even been turned on.[2]

The nurses felt betrayed, and none of these words of explanation diminished the sense that administrators did not trust them. Let's imagine that the intent of the officials who decided to set up the cameras was pure and that they were simply oblivious to the potential impact of their actions. It is possible that they truly trusted the nurses and were trying to protect them from petty theft that they believed was being perpetrated by outside intruders. Even if this were true, the nurses have to decide which story is more plausible: the story of trust, or the story of mistrust. The nurses could not see the intentions of the administrators; they could only see the outcome. The same is true for any activity you undertake. Our UCLA colleague, Kelly Bean, leads teams with her mantra that "People don't see our intentions, they see our behaviors."[3] We have to be constantly vigilant how our decisions and actions will impact trust.

Transparency Builds Trust

George Borst faced a difficult decision when he was president of Toyota Financial Services (TFS). Plagued by a tough economy, TFS needed to reorganize, and several financial service centers around the country would have to close or be consolidated. The reorganization would take two years, and Borst did not yet know which centers would be affected.

What often happens under such conditions is that the executive team isolates itself, hoping that if they don't talk about imminent scary change, then employees won't talk about it, either. Instead, when uncertainty is looming, that is all employees talk about and the rumor mill runs amok. Anyone who can jump ship and find another job does so. George needed the employee team to work diligently to keep the company afloat during the difficult transition, he wanted to retain top talent through the bumpy ride ahead, and he understood that his first task would be to show that he could be trusted.

Instead of insulating himself in a corporate cocoon, he and the executive board visited every center in the country and demonstrated transparency and trustworthiness. They told the employees that they still did not know which centers would be affected, but that the day the team made a decision would be the same day all employees would be told. They would hide nothing. For those whose centers would be closed, they would work hard to find them another job within the company. Should that not be possible for any particular employees, either because there were no opportunities, or even because an employee could not relocate due to personal issues, TFS would hire a job search firm to help them find other employment. George could not guarantee job security, but he could guarantee loyalty to his employees.

He tells us that the two years were astonishingly productive; very few employees left during the two-year period, and the transition was impressively smooth. To highlight the effect of creating the trusted relationships, not a single lawsuit was filed against the company by any employee in the transition (personal communication with George Borst, 2010).[4] As a leader, George understood the value of transparency. We can take bad news, but we really don't like to be taken by surprise. Wherever possible, keep people apprised and tell them the truth.

Vulnerability Builds Trust

When Ron Sugar began his tenure as president of Northrop Grumman, he asked the HR team to schedule a one-week leadership program for all vice presidents to meet and chart the course of the company. The HR team was fielding suggestions for a session to help the organization develop trust in its new leader. Moshe was at the planning session and shared that Ron, a UCLA graduate, played the piano; he proposed that the conference start with Ron taking the stage and, instead of moving to the podium, sitting down at a piano to play. The program organizers liked the idea, Ron agreed, and on the day of the program the reaction of the audience to the 5-minute performance was overwhelming.

What followed was even more important in establishing Ron's relationship with the team. Ron walked to the podium and told them that as a young man, he had aspired to become a composer. For the next

15 minutes, he humbly shared more about himself. Clearly, composing hadn't worked out, but he told the group that those past personal goals were not what kept him up at night anymore. Now he was concerned about ways to ensure that trust, integrity, and living up to core values would always be at the forefront of every person's behavior in the organization. It was everyone's job to chart that course; he could not do it alone.

In those first few minutes Ron made himself vulnerable, and in so doing demonstrated that he trusted the audience, gaining their trust in return. The conference was off to a remarkable start.

When you are taking the lead of a team and they don't know you, the first thing to do is establish trust. Trust has to be built, it has to be earned; it does not just happen because you have been given a title. As a team leader, initiating the conversation to identify standards creates the foundation for group trust. Living up to the standards in every action thereafter builds and solidifies that trust.

Trusting New Team Members

What if you manage a team and a new member joins? To build trust, we can break down levels of authority and delegation, creating a process to build shared trust.[5] At the most basic level, give the new person the role of gathering information for a project and reporting to the group. You will gain trust in their ability to filter and organize. From there, on the next level of authority, you can ask them to identify possible action plans and recommend an action, so you can develop trust in their ability to generate solutions and make judgments. At the third level of authority, they can design parts of the action plan, demonstrating their ability to understand detail and both analyze and synthesize facts. Once the team is comfortable with the new member at this level of authority, they can be given authority over executing the plan. Demonstrating their ability to problem-solve and adapt the plan as needed increases their trustworthiness, and you will become increasingly comfortable giving them ever greater authority.

Of course, if the new member disappoints the team at any of these levels of authority, the role of the leader will be to coach them and help them improve before giving them greater autonomy. The way a new member responds to constructive criticism will have a marked impact on the team's sense of trust as well. If you are the new member, be aware that every action you take and every reaction you have affects the team's judgment of how trustworthy you are. It takes conscious effort to build shared trust, as parents of teenagers can attest. Indeed, these same principles of building shared trust are as important for strengthening family teams as they are for work teams. Trust is built when we live up to standards and follow through on our commitments.

Gaining the Trust of Others

Has anyone ever come to you and tried to convince you of something, and then said, "Just trust me, this is going to work." Those words, "Just trust me," set off warning bells in our brains! They create psychological distance; now this is the last person you want to trust. A much more powerful way to establish trust is to show that you are trustworthy with actions, much as George Borst did when he created a concrete plan to take care of any Toyota employees affected by the consolidation.

Another powerful way to build trust is to demonstrate your trust in the person with whom you are trying to develop a relationship, as Ron Sugar did by demonstrating vulnerability. The same principle applies not only to building trust in teams, but also to enabling negotiations. At the start of negotiations to rebuild a severely damaged highway, contractor C.C. Myers told the city's mayor that he was ready to sign a two-page letter of agreement so that the work could begin immediately. Signing government contracts usually takes months, with endless revisions back and forth between teams of lawyers. Myers told the mayor that waiting for a final contract was not necessary to allow the work to begin. The implicit message to the mayor was, "I trust you. I trust that your attorneys will be fair in their negotiations with my attorneys, and we don't have to let those talks delay the start of the work."

What happens when you show someone that you trust them? In the brain of the person who feels trusted, the hormone oxytocin is released.[6] When our brains get a squirt of oxytocin, we can't help but become more trusting in that moment; you get the sense that the person in front of you is not a threat, and can be trusted. For the vice presidents at

Northrop Grumman, hearing Ron Sugar play the piano sent the message that Ron felt it was safe for him to share his personal self; they felt trusted and, in turn, sensed that he was a leader they could trust. For the mayor, hearing that the contractor was willing to start the work before a final contract was signed signaled that the contractor trusted him; the mayor judged that the contractor could also be trusted, and they were able to conclude a deal.

Trust, Economic Development, and National Well-Being

The success and well-being of entire societies is predicated on trust; trust eliminates and reduces the uncertainty inherent in the interactions between strangers, and creates greater willingness to cooperate with others. Economists studying the per capita income disparities among countries have shown a link between trustworthiness and prosperity. The World Values Survey, an annual international social survey conducted in over 100 countries, asks people, "Generally speaking, would you say that most people can be trusted, or that you need to be very careful in dealing with people?"[7] The Gallup World Poll frames the question a little differently, asking, "In the city or area where you live, imagine you lost your wallet or something holding your identification or address and it was found by someone else. Do you think your wallet (or your valuables) would be returned to you if it were found by a neighbor/the police/a stranger?" The most trustful countries have much higher per capita income; progressively lower levels of trust across countries correlate with lower levels of per capita income.[8] Trust facilitates trade, which is essential to prosperity in our universally linked world.

Per capita income is only one measure of national well-being. Governments are increasingly focusing their attention on multiple factors that affect national well-being, and evidence suggests that trust is associated with a range of positive outcomes. For example, in societies where people tend to trust each other, their democracies are stronger, crime and corruption are lower, and even health is better. Within an organization or team, high-trust groups consistently outperform low-trust groups. Higher levels of trust are also associated with higher levels of subjective satisfaction with life ("How happy are you?"), both in the workplace and in larger communities and even nations.[9]

Respect

Respect is a universal value that demonstrates your esteem for the worth and dignity of other people. There are many opportunities in every interaction to show respect, as discussed in the following sections.

Names

One of the most fundamental signs of respect is learning people's names. For example, an executive in a major corporation was about to meet a dozen top recruits for his department. These were outstanding students in their respective universities, and with a shortage of professionals in their field, they all had offers from competing companies. As each recruit came into the room, the executive greeted them and addressed them by name, with no need for introduction. The recruits were visibly surprised that he already knew their names. When he opened the floor for questions, his responses included information that showed he knew the background and experiences of the person asking the question. He had clearly taken the time to review their resumes, and had requested photos of each one and learned their names. After the meeting, the executive walked with them to the parking lot, greeting every employee they passed along the way by name. Just outside the building, maintenance workers were fixing a broken light, and the executive greeted them by name as well. Every one of these recruits chose this company as their place of employment.

Many people we know remember working for a boss who did not know their name even after months of employment with the company. One woman named Sharon was repeatedly and consistently called Susan by her boss. How committed do you think Sharon felt to this team? In contrast, what impression did those recruits get when the executive greeted everyone, including the maintenance workers, by name?

We are all incredibly sensitive to our names. In the cocktail party phenomenon, several conversations can be going on at the same time in a room. You might be engaged in one conversation, and across the room, several conversations away from you, somebody says your name. Like radar, your ears pick it up! You can't hear anything else they are saying, but you can hear your name. What happens when someone sends you a written request and misspells your name? They can misspell other words and you might be more forgiving, but if they misspell your name, your reaction is likely to be far less generous.

We can all use the excuse that it's hard to remember names, or bemoan the fact that we are particularly bad with names, but that makes knowing people's names that much more meaningful. We all recognize what an effort it takes to learn and remember names and that is precisely what makes it such a powerful sign of respect.[10]

Active Listening

When you get together with team members, whether it's a conversation with just one person or the whole team, make sure you don't do all the talking. Respect for others means that everyone should have a voice at the table. If you notice someone has not said anything, pause and ask if they have any reaction to what has transpired so far. Even if they say they agree with everyone else, you have offered them the opportunity to share their thoughts. Not every person will need or want to talk, but it should be a choice, not a default to silence because a few people are dominating the room. Try to follow a simple rule: listen twice as much as you talk. After all, you were born with two ears but one mouth, so use them proportionally! As a team member, you will earn more respect from others for your attentive listening than for the pearls of wisdom you bestow on the room.

Attentive listening is not easy, and it is even more difficult when we are always in a rush. In our zeal to speed things up, we interrupt people. We don't let them finish their thoughts. Make a point to notice if you are guilty; if you are, you will see how difficult it is at first to hold your tongue and only respond or ask your questions after you have fully processed what was said.

We also (erroneously) believe we can pay attention to more than one thing at a time, and so we try to pay continuous partial attention to many things at the same time.[11] People sit in meetings with smartphones surreptitiously held under the table, monitoring incoming e-mails even as the team is talking about something else. Others have their laptops open on the conference table, and they blatantly dart across websites as the team is discussing an issue or someone is presenting an update. We meet a colleague for lunch and sit with the phone on the table, glancing at it periodically while our friend is talking. Active listening and total engagement show respect for the people in the room. If you are checking e-mail or staring at a screen when you are with other people, the implicit message is, "You are not worthy of my full attention."

One creative way to think about when it is or is not appropriate to bring out the electronic interrupters is to imagine that you are pulling out a crossword puzzle instead.[12] Would you work on a crossword puzzle during a meeting? Would it be good manners to do a puzzle while at dinner with friends? How about in the middle of a job interview? (Yes! We have heard too many stories of job candidates actually checking their phones during an interview!) If you wouldn't do a crossword puzzle in a given setting, then it's not okay to focus on your electronic devices.

Divided Attention

We've all tried to use the excuse that we can pay attention to more than one thing at a time; that we're listening to someone talking even though we are checking e-mail at the same time. The reality is that you cannot pay attention to more than one thing at a time. No matter how smart you are, the brain just can't do it. Instead of actually focusing on two things at a time, the brain rapidly switches back and forth between them.

Try the following exercise to convince yourself that you are not an exception. Say aloud all 26 letters of the alphabet as quickly as you can. When you have finished with the letters, say aloud as quickly as you can all the numbers from 1 to 26. Now try to do these tasks together. That is, alternate between them so that you are saying aloud "A, 1, B, 2, C, 3 . . ."

How quickly did you start to make mistakes? While focusing on the numbers you lost track of the letters, and vice versa. As you try to do both, you are switching back and forth between tasks, and in the switch there are costs. You are losing information, you are making more mistakes, and you probably found yourself draining mental energy to try to pull it off. Trying to do both at the same time was more mentally exhausting than doing each task separately. Attention is a finite resource. Just as time is a limited resource that we guard with calendars and manage with planners, we have to think about managing our attention as well.

Time and Attention Management

The negative impact of divided attention is becoming more obvious as we grow increasingly tethered to sources of distraction. In 2008 a collaboration was formed called The Information Overload Research Group. One of their reports calculated that information overload costs the U.S. economy $900 billion per year in lost productivity. Intel, a member of the group, piloted a series of programs to see what might be done to promote more effective thinking in teams.[13] The experiments were variations on the theme of Quiet Time—giving people explicit license to think without having to respond to e-mails or other sources of interruption. For example, the engineers in one group were given Quiet Tuesdays over a three-month period. During Tuesday mornings, they were asked to collaborate with each other on projects and leave all electronic communications aside. Computers were set to "offline," phones were forwarded to voice mail, and "Do Not Disturb" signs were placed around their work spaces. Having license to think for 4 contiguous hours was amazing; it dramatically improved project efficiencies and effectiveness. Most of the engineers recommended extending the program to the whole organization.

To be actively engaged and think deeply about issues requires blocks of undivided attention. You will be able to think more effectively and collaborate more successfully when you actively work to attend to one thing at time. And the bonus is that people will feel respected, and respect you, when you give them this kind of space to do their best work.

Dignify the Detail Doers

Respect should be blind to age, rank, title, gender, and all attributes of diversity. It should be accorded to all with whom we come in contact. Every person in an organization has value, and we should find ways to dignify the detail doers. When the executive at the recruitment meeting greeted all the employees he passed, including the maintenance workers, and addressed them by name, he was acknowledging them overtly and implicitly sending the message, "You are valuable and worthy of my attention." When Richard Feynman revealed the purpose of the top-secret Manhattan Project to the students cranking out rote mathematical calculations, he too was treating them with dignity.

One of the surest ways to diminish respect and compromise a person's dignity is the language used to define roles. During a terrible snowstorm in the Northeast, city officials broadcast a request asking all "nonessential workers" to stay home. Who exactly is a nonessential worker? What kind of message does this label send? There are variations on this theme. In many medical organizations, the two categories of employees are Physician and Non-Physician. What is the implicit message to the Non-Physicians? To optimize a team or an organization, every member has to feel that they contribute in a meaningful way to the purpose. Names matter, titles matter, and language matters.

Equality

Disastrous outcomes in airplane cockpits and hospital operating rooms have been documented as the direct result of inequality among team participants.[14] In 1982, an Air Florida flight crashed into the Potomac River in Washington, DC. The cockpit voice recorder was recovered from the wreckage and revealed that the captain had disregarded the concerns of the first officer, who detected something wrong with the engine instruments before takeoff. The first officer had tried *six times* to suggest that something did not seem right, but the captain dismissed the concerns, did not use any of the data the first officer provided, and took off anyway. NASA research has shown that the primary cause of aviation accidents is human error, and one of the biggest factors is failure of communication.

Aviation Crew Resource Management training now emphasizes behaviors that crew members are expected to demonstrate in order to shape equality of thinking in the cockpit. These techniques have been adopted in surgical operating rooms as well, to facilitate communication between nurses and surgeons and reduce medical errors. The best idea or an important insight can come from any source, irrespective of seniority or job title.[15]

"Please" and "Thank You"

The simplest things are often the most overlooked. One of the easiest ways to create an environment of respect is to say "please" and "thank you" when you interact with your team. In our rush to meet deadlines and our distracted juggling of lots of projects at the same time, we become very abrupt with language. Requests are replaced with commands. A curt "Send me the Johnson report!" creates a different emotional response than "Could you please send me the Johnson report?" We may not realize the impact a well-placed "thank you" has on morale. Iris's daughter was working in her first corporate job after college. There was a sharp learning curve as she adjusted to the demands of the office. A few months into the job, her boss sent her an e-mail thanking her for all her hard work and for putting so much effort into the success of the team. What made it even more special was that her daughter received the e-mail on a Saturday afternoon. This leader had taken time out of her weekend to say "thank you."

Integrity

Our commitments and our actions have to be aligned. Integrity means that what you say is what you do. What happens if you have to break a promise, or you break one inadvertently? If you know you will not be able to keep a promise, inform your team as soon as possible of the circumstances and ask their counsel. If it's too late, and you have already broken a promise, fess up quickly and take steps to remedy the breach of trust you have caused. We may not always live up to our standards, but let's not make that the new standard. Integrity means we take responsibility and own up to our mistakes. Humans are not going to be flawlessly perfect. In fact, the most reliable part of any system is human unreliability.[16] People will make mistakes, and a sustainable system has to make room for error and be designed to make recovery possible. In Chapter 6, "Acknowledge, Learn, Correct," we will discuss more fully the attitude and strategy toward error that is necessary for a team to shape success in a world of uncertainty.

Empathy

Empathy is an understanding of the process of perception, and accepting that other people may not see the world the way we do. Thinking with empathy, we can discover much more about what motivates others to act as they do. To be empathetic, we have to discount our thoughts of how we think others *should* think and feel, or what *we* would think and feel were we in the same situation, and discover what they *do* think and feel. Empathy can help teams solve problems much more effectively.

As an example, Moshe was travelling in Israel with his wife and they met Ahmed, an Arab living in East Jerusalem. Ahmed posed an interesting question. "Imagine that you, your mother, your wife, and your child are in a boat, and it capsizes. You can save yourself, and only one of the other three. Who will you save?" With his wife standing next to him, Moshe had to carefully phrase his answer. He explained to Ahmed that he would save the child, because a child still has his whole future ahead of him. Ahmed told Moshe that he had failed the test. For Ahmed there was only one correct answer, which he was able to explain. "You see," he said, "you can have more than one child in a lifetime, and you can have more than one wife, but you will only have one mother. You must save your mother!" What was so obvious to Ahmed would not have occurred to us.[17]

Diversity

How is it that people see the world so differently? At birth, we all have similar 1-pound brains, but by the time we are adults, our brains weigh 3 pounds. Those extra 2 pounds of brain that we gain as we go through life hold the answer. At birth, we have billions of brain cells that are just waiting to start working. Each brain cell can connect with up to 10,000 other brain cells, by developing spindles that reach out to other cells (imagine each brain cell is like an octopus with up to 10,000 tentacles). These connections are formed based on the experiences you have; every experience creates new connections. For example, remember the story of Coach K and the U.S. Olympic basketball team from the beginning of the book? What medal did the devastated team from the 2004 Olympics bring back to the United States? If you did not know before reading this book but you can name it now, your brain has undergone a structural change. You now have a network of connections that form your memory of the story. This means that our brains are changing every minute of our lives (yes, even in sleep!). All these connections that are formed based on our experiences act as filters to help us understand, interpret, and predict the outside world. Because each of us has had a different set of experiences, we each have a different set of connections, and we each perceive the world differently.

Empathy: Thinking inside the Other Person's Box

A participant in one of our courses, who had served in the military in Afghanistan, described the difficulty that village women have obtaining clean drinking water. The women have to walk for miles with their water pots, returning with their heavy loads on foot. Without easy access to clean water, illness and mortality rates among villagers were appalling. The U.S. military decided to solve the problem by digging wells in each village, a simple solution that would seemingly make life better for all. To their amazement, as soon as the wells were ready, the women would destroy them. What could motivate such behavior? It was incomprehensible until they looked at it from the perspective of the women.

It turned out that for these women, the journey to the remote water sources held much more meaning than the well diggers understood. For women in this culture, the only way to get permission from the men to leave the village was to get water. Walking to the distant water sources, they would stop at other villages and sell small items to earn a little money; on the way back, they would stop to rest with their heavy loads and enjoy the company of women in other villages, sharing information with them. The new wells were cutting off a source of income, a source of information, and a source of friendship.

Closer to home, a middle school principal was wrestling with a makeup ritual that some of the preteen girls had started. They were applying lipstick in the school bathroom and then kissing the mirror, creating a mess. The principal understood that the best way to get the girls to stop smudging the mirror would not be through threats but rather to understand what would make them want to stop. Thinking empathetically, she found her solution. She invited the girls to come watch the janitor remove the lipstick marks from the mirror. With the girls watching, the janitor took out his squeegee, dipped it into a toilet, and proceeded to clean the mirror. As you can imagine, that was the last day any lipstick marks appeared!

Inclusion

A university was celebrating the inauguration of a new dean on a rooftop patio. There were many invited dignitaries, donors, and friends at the party. Moshe noticed that a mutual friend, Azriel, was absent. He asked the dean why Azriel was not there, and he responded, "I didn't invite him because the event is on the roof, and given his ill health I knew he wouldn't be able to climb the stairs. I didn't want him to feel obliged to come."

Later that week, Moshe went to visit their ailing friend. Azriel already knew that he had not been invited to the gala and he was crushed. Moshe tried to make him feel better and told him that the dean had thought it would be in his best interest not to come. Azriel slumped in his armchair, shook his head, and said, "He should have let me decide."

The Pain of Exclusion

Excluding people is the ultimate insult. Excluding them by not inviting them to a meeting, or ignoring them if they are in the meeting, builds psychological walls and barriers that make effective collaboration difficult if not impossible. Recent research in social neuroscience shows just how powerful social rejection can be. If you ask people to recall some of their earliest negative experiences, they usually bring up events of rejection—not being invited to a birthday party, nobody wanting to sit next to them on the school bus, being picked last for a team. Naomi Eisenberger at UCLA has looked at the brain scans of people experiencing social rejection and has found something remarkable.[18] The areas of the brain that are activated when we experience social pain are the same areas that are activated when we experience physical pain. To the brain, intense feelings of rejection really do feel like being socked in the stomach.

The research underscores that the hurt feelings of rejection are serious. From an evolutionary perspective there is even good reason for feelings of social rejection to be so painful.[19] From the days of the hunter-gatherers our survival has depended on collaboration; fending off wild animals and hunting for food required teamwork. To make individual weakness irrelevant and to benefit from the strength of the tribe, members needed to behave in ways that would keep everyone happy. Any deviant behavior that threatened the group would lead to ejection and exclusion. The pain associated with rejection would become an evolutionary advantage as an internal mechanism to stop people from deviant behaviors.

Even brief, seemingly meaningless incidents of exclusion can hurt. In one study, when participants passed a stranger who seemed to look right through them rather than making eye contact, they felt less social connection and more isolated than those with whom the stranger made eye contact.[20] If a stranger can do this to us, no wonder we feel upset at a cocktail party when the person we are talking to is looking past our ear and scanning the room, instead of paying attention to us. Other research has found that even being excluded by a group we dislike can make us feel left out, so it should come as no surprise that being ignored by colleagues can have at least as large an effect.

When you manage large groups, there may be times that smaller meetings of subgroups are needed. It is important to make it clear that nobody is ever excluded on a personal level, and they are welcome to join if they want to be part of the conversation. When in doubt, include. Wherever possible, don't make the decision for them. Compromising inclusion can be devastating to the team spirit, performance, and potential for acting together into the future. Make a note to take the pulse of the room even when a meeting gets started; take a good look around and ask others whether anyone is not present who should have been included. It's not too late to right a wrong.

Communication

A pervasive complaint in organizations is a lack of communication. More communication, however, is not the core problem; what we need is more *effective* communication.

Clarity

Read the following paragraph and see if you can make any sense of it. Imagine that your boss gave you these instructions and told you to lead the team and make it happen. Would you have any idea what to do?

> The procedure is actually quite simple. First, you arrange things into different groups, depending on their makeup. Of course, one pile may be sufficient, depending on how much there is to do. If you have to go somewhere else due to lack of facilities, that is the next step. Otherwise, you are pretty well set. It is important not to overdo any particular endeavor. That is, it is better to do too few things at once than too many. In the short run this may not seem important, but complications from doing too many can easily arise. A mistake can be expensive as well. The manipulation of the appropriate mechanism should be self-explanatory.[21]

How many meetings do you go to that sound like this? You know it's English, but it makes no sense at all, except perhaps to the person talking. George Bernard Shaw once quipped that "the biggest problem with communication is the illusion it has occurred."

In the preceding instructions, two words would have made understanding possible. The paragraph provided instructions for washing clothes. Now that you know that the context is laundry, reread the paragraph and observe what your mind is able to do with the information that you could not do before.

How will you ever know whether your communications are coming across like the first version of the paragraph? You think you have just given an epic speech, only to discover much later that nobody knew what you were talking about. Effective communication can be facilitated by the following three rules.

Open with a Hook   Start with the headline. What is the key message for the audience? The hook makes them care about what you are going to say next. Learning how to find the hook in a message, Nora Ephron tells the story of her first writing assignment in her high school journalism class. The teacher asked the class to write the lead sentence for an article with the following facts:

> Ken Peters, principal of Beverly Hills High School, announced today that the entire high school faculty will travel to Sacramento next Thursday for a colloquium in new teaching methods. Among the speakers will be anthropologist Margaret Mead, college president Dr. Robert Smith, and California governor Pat Brown.

Ephron and most of the students produced leads that reworded the facts in some way. The teacher told them there was really only one important message to the students who would be reading the article, and that should be the lead: *There will be no school next Thursday!*[22]

Move from the General to the Specific   Too often we jump right into cryptic detail, assuming that other people know what we already know. After the hook, continue by setting the stage with a broad overview— your issue as it would be presented in *USA Today*. Then you can dive in with the kind of specific detail you would find in a more comprehensive journal—the *Scientific American* coverage of your story.

Ask for Questions   During your presentation you can ask, "Does anyone have any questions?" but who in the room wants to be the person who says they haven't a clue what you are talking about? A tactic that both of us have adopted is to ask our students, "Please let me know if I am not being clear." The implicit message is that if anyone in the group is confused, we, as speaker, accept the responsibility for the lack of clarity. We have found students to be much more willing to ask questions for clarification.

Tell a Story

Communication shouldn't be thought of as "information transfer" from one person to another, like passing water between buckets. This thinking assumes that the second bucket is passive, and starts out empty.

Instead, listeners already have a huge store of information. The most effective communication uses stories to tap into knowledge the listener already has, and helps them use that information to connect with the message. For example, suppose a leader wants to inspire a team that they can create value despite the constraints of limited resources, and tells the following story:

> The inventive capacity of people to create extraordinary outcomes with limited resources is astonishing. Consider, for example, the Giza pyramid. The ancient Egyptians had no heavy construction equipment, yet the pyramid contains more than two million boulders, they each weigh more than two tons, and the height of the pyramid is equal to a 30-story building. It was built 5,000 years ago and remained the tallest manmade structure on earth for thousands of years, until the Eiffel Tower was built in 1889.

With this story we tap into your preexisting knowledge about Egyptian pyramids and connect it to the leadership message in a novel way. It gets us thinking that if the Egyptians could build something so impressive with limited resources 5,000 years ago, let's see what we can do.

Similarly, effective communicators often use analogies and metaphors, which are types of stories that connect known things in new ways, as a powerful means of communication and as a trigger for idea generation. For example, Thomas Stemberg, the cofounder of Staples, stimulated thinking in the early stages of his company's development by asking, "Could we be the Toys 'R' Us of office supplies?" Stemberg used the analogy to help his team imagine a novel future for the office supply business.[23]

Injecting something new into a familiar story is also an effective tool for communication. For example, when you get on an airplane, you expect the usual safety speech from the flight attendant (is there really anyone on an airplane who doesn't know how to fasten a seat belt?). It's so familiar that nobody pays attention. To break the known pattern, Southwest Airlines encourages their flight attendants to use humor and novelty—and people listen specifically to hear what will be different.

Stories Keep Our Attention

Effective communication requires that the listener be curious. A good hook sparks curiosity, but we have to keep it alive with our story. Curiosity happens when we feel a gap in our knowledge between what we know and what we want to know. If we know absolutely nothing about the topic, or can't connect what is being communicated to what we know, the gap becomes a chasm, the experience is like reading the washing-clothes description, and we tune out. If we already know everything, like the airplane safety spiel, there is no gap at all, and we also tune out.[24]

We tend to tell people the facts, but first we have to make them curious about them. News program teaser ads do this brilliantly. "What lethal food might be on your breakfast table?! Join us for News at 11:00!" A great story demonstrates a gap by highlighting some specific knowledge meaningful to the listener that they are missing, and then closing the gap. Think about how you share information with your team. Are you the airline safety announcement? How can you use stories to better connect with people?

The PowerPoint Curse

A recent Google search turned up 3,760,000 results for the phrase "Death by PowerPoint," and Google Images has lots of cartoons making fun of the presentations that all of us dread. So, a moment of truth— when someone speaks while flashing slides inundated with data and overloaded with words, do you mentally check out? Given what we know about the brain and divided attention, it makes perfect sense to tune the whole thing out. The brain can only pay attention to one thing at a time. You can either listen to the speaker or read the slides, but not both at the same time. Toggling back and forth between listening and reading takes too much cognitive effort, so we do neither, and start thinking of the work waiting for us after the meeting.

There is a better way! At the extreme, some organizations have eliminated all PowerPoint at meetings. For example, no PowerPoint is allowed in staff meetings at Amazon. None. Instead, meetings start with a white paper, a narrative memo of background, context, and ideas that the presenter wants to discuss in the conversation that follows.[25] Jeff

Bezos, CEO of Amazon, understands that people don't have time to read before the meeting, so those gathered get quiet reading time before the conversation starts. The real value of a meeting is to share ideas and think together about the tough issues, not to drown each other in data.

An executive VP at a top defense company took our advice to try three months of meetings with no PowerPoint. He was amazed at the result. Participants became far more engaged, better ideas on the tough issues were generated, and meetings took less time.

One of the most serious dangers of PowerPoint is the misplaced aura of certainty it can create. The report of the Columbia Accident Investigation Board included an analysis of the way information was shared within NASA while the space shuttle *Columbia* was in orbit, damaged but still intact. One of the criticisms was the way a crucial piece of information was handled. An important engineering detail was buried in a sea of PowerPoint data, crowded in a small font on a slide with too many bullet points. This crucial information might have been noticed and disaster averted had it been presented as part of a white paper and thus engaged discussion.[26]

There may certainly be occasions when PowerPoint as a vehicle to display data or as a visual aid is warranted. Our caution is to think judiciously about when that should be.

Conversation Stoppers

Mark Twain aptly said that "most conversation is a monologue in the presence of witnesses." In such cases there is no learning or new thinking developing in any of the brains involved. Every team should consider: when we get together, how do we talk to each other? The word *conversation* comes from the root *converse*, meaning "opposite." In a conversation, people who do not think alike, and who may have completely opposing views, learn from each other.

When it comes to exploring new ideas, we overestimate ourselves; we believe we are more open minded than the average person, and more open minded than we actually are. In fact, our brains prefer familiar, safe patterns and comfortable, well-known routines. New ideas carry risk, which our evolutionary survival-focused brains can't help but resist. What happens when a colleague suggests a totally new possibility, something that has never been tried before? When a new idea is presented to us, we cannot help but see its potential flaws and pitfalls. The amygdala, the brain's fear-response center, is activated and screams, "No!" even as we generously say, "Sure, let's discuss it." The amygdala is housed in the limbic system, a much more primitive and powerful part of the brain than the rational cortex. Designed to help us survive imminent threats and initiate an immediate response to danger, the amygdala can overwhelm the cortex, which might want to reason through the situation. From an evolutionary view this imbalance makes a lot of sense—in the face of an angry tiger growling outside the cave, our savanna-roaming ancestors would be dead if the amygdala let the curious cortex lead them outside to get more data on the threat. The amygdala operates under the principle of "better safe than sorry." What is familiar feels safer than the unknown, and so we have an inertia-like tendency to stick with what we know, and maintain the status quo.

Just say YO

While we may think that we are open minded to new ideas, what generally happens to most of us is that we suppress our initial desire to say no. We don't say yes; perhaps we hedge just enough to give ourselves time to develop a good argument so that we can later say no in a tactful way. The reality is that a new idea may have flaws. Think of a new idea as a newborn infant. Have you ever gone to a maternity ward to visit new parents and taken a good look at the babies there? Every parent thinks their infant is perfect, but as visitors, we can't help but see flaws: unruly hair, a cone-shaped head, a squashed nose. Same with a new idea; we can't help but see the imperfections because they are there—the idea is in its infancy. However, just as an infant needs time to develop to show its potential, so does a new idea. If we say no too quickly, we never allow the idea to mature and its potential to emerge.

So, how might we best respond to a new idea? Saying no too quickly cuts off any possibility, but with the flaws apparent in the idea, you are not ready to say yes. You could say "maybe," but that usually means a slow no! Our language lacks a word that effectively balances yes *and* no. We invented a neutral word that is between yes and no: YO.[27] Any new idea, suggestion, or proposal deserves to get the benefit of the doubt. With YO, you grant yourself the freedom to journey down new mental paths, to digest possibilities, and to explore possible options that you otherwise might never consider.

Fluidity

How easy is it for team members to communicate with one another? Do people have access, in real time, to the information they need to make good decisions and smart moves? Southwest Airlines prides itself on superb team collaboration. The heart of their success is an emphasis on communication that is frequent and timely. Compared to other airlines, Southwest consistently has the fastest gate turnarounds in the industry. Other airlines struggle because ground time between landing and the next departure is complex, requiring the efforts of at least 12 functions (pilots, flight attendants, mechanics, gate agents, ticketing agents, ramp agents, baggage transfer agents, cleaners, caterers, fuelers, freight, and operations agents). Uniquely, at Southwest all these functions share information; everyone knows everything about what's happening when the plane is on the ground, and they can respond quickly and effectively to changing circumstances. When problems arise, instead of pointing fingers to fix blame, Southwest employees are encouraged to report widely and immediately, so that everyone can get involved in figuring out a solution.[28]

Standards Are Unique to Each Team

The U.S. Olympic basketball team decided that the standards of respect for their team would include looking one another in the eye when talking. There are cultures in which looking another person in the eye is actually a signal of disrespect. In various Asian, African, and Latin American cultures, prolonged eye contact is considered rude. This is a great example of how every team has to build its own standards. Part of the conversation, then, is to learn what is important to other team members and to remember that cultural differences need to surface. Coach K has a conversation about standards with every new team he works with. Colleagues at work are not the only teams to benefit from establishing standards. Parents find this a very effective tool to improve relationships with children, and social groups find that friendships are deepened through the process. While core values are universal, the standards that matter to a team will be unique, reflecting the distinctive needs and composition of the team itself.

■ ■ ■

Creating an identity steeped in a clearly articulated and compelling purpose and establishing standards are requirements for effective collaboration. In the next chapter, we will discuss principles that foster commitment, build resilience, and breathe life into the standards.

4

AMPLIFY THE POSITIVE

Foster Resilience, Engagement, and Sustainable Change

ACCORDING TO THE 2013 GALLUP STATE OF THE AMERICAN WORKPLACE REPORT, 70 percent of U.S. workers are either "not engaged" or "actively disengaged" at work. Only 30 percent are "enthusiastic about, and committed to their work and contribute to their organization in a positive manner." Fifty-two percent of workers say they are essentially "checked out" at work, and 18 percent report being so miserable that they actively undermine the efforts of their more engaged coworkers. You might think that these numbers are related to the economic tensions of the Great Recession, but they have barely changed since Gallup started tracking them in 2000.[1]

Creating a culture that is focused on purpose, igniting the frame of mind to thrive, and building on the strengths of individuals, teams, and organizations are essential for creating value and shaping the future. In this chapter we describe the process for motivating engagement and creating the commitment and resilience needed to achieve extraordinary outcomes.

Breathe Life into Standards

Creating standards is important, but just creating the standards is no guarantee that they will ever be integrated into your behavior. Just think about New Year's resolutions. You promise yourself that this year it will be different, that you are really going to change. You vow that you will go to the gym every Saturday, stop eating salty snack foods, watch less reality TV, and call your brother every Sunday. Now it's a Saturday in the middle of February and you are on the couch, not at the gym. In fact, you have only been to the gym twice since the year started. You have watched 4 hours of (fill in your reality TV addiction here), you have eaten two large bags of BBQ-flavored potato chips, and the thought occurs to you that you haven't called your brother for three weeks. Clearly, it's not enough just to make a list of standards and vow that this time we mean it.

If standards are the behaviors we want to live up to, as individuals and as teams, how do we breathe life into them?

Celebrate Daily

To strengthen and actualize behaviors, *celebrate them daily*. We can borrow a page from the Ritz-Carlton Hotel Company to see how this is done in a team. At the Ritz-Carlton, every employee in the entire hotel chain gathers with their team for a 15-minute "lineup" each morning. The purpose of the lineup is to reinforce the company's values. Each day is dedicated to one of the values, and people in each team lineup are asked to offer what the value means to them, what they are doing to live up to the value, and to share a story if they have seen a good example of the value on the job. In addition, a "wow" story is chosen from among the team lineups and shared throughout the entire chain, across all the hotels in every country. Each day's story is about a staff person who went above and beyond to create the magical service that defines the Ritz. The purpose of the story is to celebrate the employee's commitment to exemplary service in front of the entire organization, and again to reinforce a value. At a deeper level, the Ritz is creating a common language and mind-set within a context of accountability.[2]

The Daily Huddle

Aruna Raghavan is the customer experience head for the Asia Pacific arm of Citigroup. In 2007, she deployed a similar program at Citigroup Singapore, and with the success in her region has since deployed the program in nearly 25 countries.[3] Financial institutions are highly analytic organizations, so at first some bankers were skeptical and did not see the point of such a seemingly touchy-feely meeting, particularly groups in the back office. But the Asia Pacific area CEO repeatedly said, "If there is anybody in this company that believes their work does not touch our customer in some way . . ." And the unstated sentiment was clear.

Teams across the bank meet daily for a 10-minute "huddle" to discuss the value of the day. There is no rank in the huddle and leadership is rotated daily so that every member gets to lead a discussion that brings a value to life. With the distributed leadership that changes every day, the implicit added message is that every single person is a significant contributor to the success of the team and the organization. Jonathan Larsen, CEO of Citibank in Singapore, commented that "in some large organizations, the staff doesn't tend to get together very frequently; we found that having this daily process creates a rhythm and rapport. It's informal, it's fun, it's a fabulous way to start out the day, and it's changed our employee dynamic."[4]

The purpose of the daily huddle is not just about customers. People don't even need to have customers to benefit from a daily huddle. Some parents have begun using a daily huddle with their children to create deeper family ties.[5]

Every team, anywhere, can organize and benefit from a 10-minute daily huddle. Pull out your list of standards. Rotate among them each day so that you focus only on one, and when you get to the end of the list, start over. If you have 10 standards, it will take you 10 days to get through them and then repeat the process. Have the team discuss three questions:

1. What does this standard mean to me?
2. What am I doing to live up to this standard?
3. Have I seen a good example of this standard on the team?

Coach K worked with his NBA players over a period of three summers to prepare for the 2008 Olympics. Once they arrived at the training camp, he and the players gathered in a hotel meeting room before every single practice. Some of the meetings were only 5 minutes long, but they were an integral part of solidifying the team identity. He notes that had the players merely assembled on the team bus and driven to the practice arena, they would be starting out the day on different wavelengths. With the daily morning meeting in the hotel before boarding the bus, they arrived at the practice site with one mind. He found these meetings to be more important than he originally expected, and they were key in strengthening the team's identity, encouraging a focus on standards, and inspiring collaboration.[6]

Celebrating a standard every day is equally effective at the individual level. Imagine the benefit of spending a few minutes at the same time each day focused on one personal standard that is important to you and asking, "What have I done this week to live up to this standard?" By celebrating daily we make ourselves more accountable and more likely to bring our best selves forward.

Chance Favors the Prepared Mind

Louis Pasteur, nineteenth-century pioneer of the germ theory of disease and inventor of pasteurization, said that "chance favors the prepared mind." He meant that insights don't happen in a vacuum; they are the fruits of diligently calibrated, directed, and attuned mind-sets. Twentieth-century cognitive psychologists have since provided ample evidence that Pasteur was right. To shape success into the future, we have to get our minds and our brains in shape to do so.

Priming

Imagine if each day *everyone* in an organization spent the first 10 minutes in the morning talking about the same standard. Knowing that everyone else also had the conversation might very well influence their interactions throughout the day. Coach K called it being on the same wavelength; in the jargon of cognitive psychologists, we would say that all minds would be *primed* to think as one.

Outside Influences

Priming is a phenomenon that makes it more likely that you will respond in a particular way if you have been exposed to a particular stimulus, which is called the *prime*. A prime is like a filtering lens, bringing certain things into greater focus, and what is extraordinary is that it can impact both thinking and behavior, and works whether we are aware of the prime or not.

For example, Yale professor John Bargh, a prominent researcher of priming, showed that subjects reading words related to old age (e.g., *gray, bingo, wrinkle*) walked more slowly when they left the study room than subjects who had read words not related to age.[7] Other studies have shown similar effects. In a game study, people behaved more competitively in the presence of a briefcase and cooperated more in the presence of a backpack.[8]

Can priming a mind-set influence more stable attributes, like math ability or voting preferences? The answer is yes. In one study, Asian American women completed a math test after responding to questions designed to either prime their ethnic identity, their gender identity, or neither identity (the control group). This study was particularly interesting because one identity (female) is stereotypically negatively associated with math performance while the other (Asian) is positively associated with math ability. If the identity questions had no influence, all groups should have had similar scores on the math test. But that's not what happened. Those primed to think about their ethnicity performed better than the control group and those primed to think about their gender performed worse than the control group.[9]

In a real-world demonstration of priming, in Arizona's 2000 general election, voters were more likely to support a sales tax to fund education if their polling location was a school, as opposed to other types of polling locations, and the effect held even when the researchers controlled for political views, party affiliation, and other demographics.[10]

Priming Ourselves

In these examples, the primes that influenced behavior were from outside influences. Can we prime ourselves? We can, in a number of beneficial ways.

Mental Practice Primes   One effective type of priming is imagining or anticipating an action by running through it in our minds. When Iris was an undergraduate in the UCLA Psychology Department, John Wooden, the legendary basketball coach, agreed to participate in a study to test the effect of mental practice on athletic success. Students who had never played basketball were recruited for the study and given coaching advice by Wooden to learn how to score a basket from the free throw line. After these lessons, the students were divided into two groups. One group came to the court for six weeks to physically practice shooting the ball. The other group never got any additional physical practice, but for the same six weeks they were guided with mental imagery techniques to imagine their movements as they shot the ball into the basket.

At the end of the six weeks, all students were evaluated to see how many baskets they could score. Astonishingly, both groups improved, and both groups improved equally. The deliberate and detailed mental practice was as effective as the physical practice. Neuroscience research in the last few years has corroborated the finding.[11] People who learn to play a song on the piano develop particular changes in the brain; when other music students just sit in front of the piano and visually imagine themselves playing the same notes, the same brain changes occur. Mentally going through the motions changes and restructures the brain as effectively as physically going through the actions. Indeed, one of the factors differentiating good athletes from exceptional athletes is the amount of mental practice in which they engage.

Emotional Primes   Can we also prime ourselves to feel differently? Charles Darwin thought so, observing that "even the simulation of an emotion tends to arouse it in our minds."[12] William James, patriarch of all psychology, wrote, "Smooth the brow, brighten the eye, contract the dorsal rather than the ventral aspect of the frame, and speak in a major key, pass the genial compliment, and your heart must be frigid indeed if it does not gradually thaw!"[13] Writing in the language of the 1800s, he was telling us to "fake it 'til you make it!"

The Smile Prime   When we feel happy we smile, but Darwin and James suggest that it can work the other way around—that forcing a smile can put us in a better mood. Psychologists have tested the idea and found it actually works. In general, smiling makes a person feel more positive and frowning makes a person feel more negative. In an interesting set of studies, Botox injections to freeze the frowning muscles has been shown to relieve symptoms of depression in a significant number of patients who underwent the treatment, compared to depressed patients receiving a placebo.[14] Our facial muscles send messages to the brain; a smile stimulates a dopamine response and boosts serotonin, two neurotransmitters that modulate a sense of well-being. Among other things, dopamine drives us to goal-driven behavior that pushes us to follow through and complete activities, while serotonin brings out feelings of satisfaction.[15]

At the same time, smiling leads to lower levels of cortisol and adrenaline, hormones that are produced in response to stress and that are toxic when our bodies are chronically awash in them. Even a disease-fighting protein called interferon gamma is produced as an effect of smiling, as well as an increase of white blood cells, which improve our immune functions. Amazing that a simple smile can prompt a chain of events that can help us feel good, improve our ability to cope with stress, and also impact long-term health.[16]

What could be a simple way to ignite a positive emotion and start this impressive chain? Plaster a smile on your face and hold it. You can do it sitting in the car, at your desk, washing dishes, anywhere and anytime. Interestingly, the effect can be enhanced by looking at yourself in the mirror. Think about how you start the day; you're in the bathroom every morning in front of a mirror. While combing your hair, try something as simple as smiling at yourself! The smile prime will help you to bring your best self to every challenge.

Other Physical Primes Traditional body language research has studied the impression our gestures and postures have on the way other people perceive us. In an interesting twist, Harvard researcher Amy Cuddy studies the impact of space-occupying physical gestures of power (e.g., outstretched arms, open chest) on the feelings, behaviors, and hormone levels of the person making the gestures. She has found that "faking" body postures associated with power—for even just 2 minutes—increases a person's testosterone, decreases their cortisol, and causes them to perform better in job interviews.[17] Next time you have the opportunity, observe the usual posture of people sitting in the lobby of an office, waiting for a meeting. Most are folded into themselves, legs crossed, head down, torso hunched over, scrolling a smartphone or looking at their hands in their lap. Cuddy offers people another alternative: start with a "power pose." If you are about to go into a tough situation like an interview, competition, or negotiation, go into a restroom stall for a little privacy, and stand tall, hands on hips, shoulders pulled back, head held high—think Superman. Hold the pose for just 2 minutes and remarkable things start to happen. You don't have to continue holding the Superman pose; after 2 minutes your brain is already primed and you will feel more confident. Then go out to the lobby and sit in a chair with body language that says, "I belong here." The body language pose isn't for other people; the message is to prime your own brain.

Thinking Primes   The voice in our head is never quiet. We are always thinking; even dreaming is a form of thinking in another biochemical state. What kinds of statements do you make to yourself? Most of us are impossibly judgmental ("Why did I do that?" "I am such a jerk." "How could I have been so stupid?" "How did I not see that coming?"). We "woulda, shoulda, coulda" all over ourselves. How often do you give yourself a mental pat on the back, an honest compliment, any words of encouragement? We tend to be nicer to our friends than we are to ourselves. Try being kinder to yourself. At the very least, at the end of each day, compliment yourself on one thing you like about yourself, one thing you feel good that you did that day, one way you lived up to your standards. Small compliments add up and you will start to expand your view of yourself as a person who can succeed.

Voices on teams are never silent, either. We are always telling ourselves stories and in every organization there are certain stories that get repeated. We frame our interpretation of data and the decisions we make based on the stories we tell ourselves. There are two types of stories that prime different kinds of thinking.

1. *Hero Stories Inspire Us*

   "OK guys, remember the time we figured out why the software was crashing?! We stuck with it and we got it! We can do this!!"

   The typical hero story tells of a heroic gamble that paid off. Amazon might share the story of a distribution center manager, eight months pregnant, who worked through the night with her team so children got their toys in time for Christmas.

   Hero stories prime us to think how to move forward.

2. *Failure Stories Warn Us*

   "Okay, guys, remember the time we couldn't find the source of the product defect and gave up? Two hundred thousand products had to be recalled! We can't let that happen again, so let's be careful this time!"

   Failure stories mainly say, "Don't do this!" They are cautionary tales about how and why terrible things happened in the past.

   The weakness of the failure story is that it primes fear and anxiety, emotions that shut down creative and expansive thinking. Failure stories get people worried, but rarely generate innovative thinking and positive action towards success.

Priming does not mean that we deny or ignore weaknesses and uncertainty, or chant vacuous positive affirmations that everything will be perfect. We will have much to say in later chapters about *acknowledging and correcting error,* and developing a system of *adaptive planning* to navigate the unexpected and uncertain elements of the unfolding future. The point of priming is that we approach every situation with some sort of mind-set, so take the opportunity to actively create the mind-set most conducive to success.

From Behavior to Habit: Repetition Matters

Do we really have to lineup, huddle, or meet daily? Isn't weekly enough? How about once a month? Or can we just tell some heartwarming stories about people living up to the standards at the annual all-hands meeting? The psychological and neuroscience research on how to turn a behavior into a habit, thereby creating sustainable change, is quite emphatic: repetition matters. Behaviors become habits when they are so ingrained we hardly have to think about them anymore. When you learn to drive, every move of your foot from the gas pedal to the brake, every shift of your gaze from windshield to mirrors, and every transfer of your hands from the steering wheel to the signals has to be consciously coordinated. You have to focus intently to get everything working together. Each time you drive it gets a little easier, until one day driving seems like an effortless choreography of motion. The driving behaviors have become habit.

When behaviors become habit, what is going on in the brain? Think of each behavior as having a corresponding network of pathways in the brain. As we noted in Chapter 3, each brain cell reaches out to other brain cells, and the web of possible connections is enormous. Once the connections are formed, the brain cells can communicate with one another, exchanging electrochemical messages to regulate behavior.

Brain cells form connections with one another based on our experiences, and learning to drive creates a web of connections linked to the driving behaviors. In the beginning, behaviors are difficult because the neural connections are being established. Once pathways are formed, every time you engage in the behavior, the signal strength of that pathway gets stronger and swifter; the electrochemical messaging system gets more fluid and faster. With added repetitions, the brain "recognizes" the behavior as matching a known pattern, and the increasingly familiar pattern of neural connections activates more easily. The fascinating part of this, according to scientists who study the brain, is that as a behavior becomes a habit, the brain uses fewer resources, in terms of less glucose and oxygen needed to fire up the pathway, corresponding to our experience of not thinking about the behavior as intently. This leaves more cognitive resources available for thinking about other things while we are acting out the habit. So, we can drive while also holding a conversation with a passenger, something that would have been difficult to do during the learning phase—or in brain language, during the phase that the neural network was consolidating.[18]

Like learning to drive, the same becomes true for standards of behaviors. At first new standards may seem awkward, and we have to think about what they mean to us and how to live up to them. It will be especially difficult if living up to a standard means that we also have to stop doing something else that has become a habit. For example, if our standard is to give one another undivided attention in meetings, we may have to break the habit of checking our phones for e-mail every few minutes (a habit most of us have perfected!).

Learning new behaviors and unlearning old ones takes cognitive effort, but with repetition less and less effort is required. Checking in daily on standards, even for 10 minutes, strengthens our neural pathways for the new habits and primes us to look for opportunities to exercise them throughout the day. The daily lineup, huddle, or Coach K–type morning meeting creates a common mind-set and a common language. By repeating the process daily, we more quickly get to the point where the standards become habit and we can more confidently count on ourselves and on the team. We can then dedicate our cognitive resources to creating extraordinary results with our teams, instead of having to think so much about team dynamics.

Positive Deviance

The purpose of the daily huddle is an informal, affirmative celebration of a standard. The focus is on a positive story or example to surface what the team is already doing. The idea is an outgrowth of a very powerful approach to creating sustainable change and shaping the future, a process called Positive Deviance. The Positive Deviance approach is a focus on assets, not deficits; looking for what is going right, instead of what is going wrong. When successful behaviors are identified, the goal is to amplify them throughout the system, and in so doing, to squeeze out the negative.

The concept of Positive Deviance started in nutrition research. In the 1990s, Tufts University professor Marian Zeitlin documented "positive deviant" children in poor communities who were better nourished than other children, despite having no additional access to resources that could account for the difference. She advocated the idea that childhood malnutrition could be combated by identifying what was different for the thriving children and then spreading those practices into the rest of the community, instead of the traditional approach that focused on what was going wrong in the community and trying to fix it.[19]

Jerry Sternin, director of the group Save the Children, and his wife, Monique, decided to use the approach to help severely malnourished children in rural Vietnam. In the first villages that they visited, they engaged with the locals and found a few children from extremely poor families who seemed to be thriving. If these very poor families in the village had well-nourished children, it meant that the same could be possible for other families in the village.

Upon close investigation, they noted that the parents of these children were gathering the same meager amount of rice as other families, but unlike other parents, they were not washing the rice. The few bugs and green weeds that got cooked into the rice provided just enough protein and vitamins to improve the nutrition of their children. Conventional village wisdom held that bugs and weeds were dangerous for young children, but these families would be able to demonstrate otherwise to the community. In addition, most families fed their young children only twice a day, before the parents went into the rice fields to work, and then again when they returned. The positive-deviant families were feeding their children exactly the same amount of rice, but four or five times a day, in smaller portions more easily digested by a small stomach.

These families were the positive deviants; positive because they were doing something that was working and deviants because they were engaged in behaviors that most in their community were not doing. Once the anomalies were found, these parents were encouraged to become trainers for the transformation of other families. Within two years, 80 percent of the children were no longer malnourished; within four years, the figure had climbed to 90 percent. Because the solution came from wisdom already within the community, members were able to sustain the behaviors without a mandate from anyone on the outside, and to shape their own path to success.[20]

The seemingly overwhelming problem of childhood malnutrition in Vietnam was conquered with positive deviance, but the method can be used for all types of problems. For example, since 1847 it has been known that in hospitals, lax medical staff hygiene spreads infection among patients. The discovery was made by Ignaz Semmelweis, a Hungarian obstetrician practicing in Vienna, who had two clinics in his maternity hospital. In the clinic for affluent women, delivery rooms were opulently furnished with heavy drapes and thick upholstery, doctors attended the births, and the incidence of infection and death was frighteningly high. In contrast, in the clinic for poor women, rooms were sparsely furnished, midwives attended the births, and somehow infection and mortality rates were far lower. Semmelweis made the connection that the doctors, unlike the midwives, were dividing their work between the delivery wards and the autopsy ward. He theorized that the doctors were bringing in cadaver germs that both rubbed off on the fabrics in the room, subsequently infecting patients through their respiratory systems when the drapes were moved, and infecting the mothers directly through skin-to-skin contact. Using the clinic for poor women as his model of positive deviance, he remodeled the opulent delivery rooms, removing the heavy fabrics, and revamped procedure so that doctors had to wash their hands with an antiseptic solution before contact with each patient. Childbirth mortality in the clinic for affluent women fell dramatically, from 18 percent to 2.2 percent.[21]

More than 150 years have passed since Semmelweis, and we have a great deal of well-documented evidence that hygiene is crucial to patient outcomes, yet 1 out of every 20 patients hospitalized in the United States gets a hospital-acquired infection, and up to 98,000 Americans die from these infections every year.[22] Transmitted by the touch of skin, clothing, or equipment, medical workers know how to prevent infection, yet top-down mandated rules are not working.

Everyone knows what they should be doing but too few comply. Hospitals have tried all sorts of aggressive strategies to improve hygiene compliance, with limited success. Despite years of hospital campaigns to increase hand washing, benchmarking best-practice programs, and other quality improvement initiatives, death rates from antibiotic-resistant bacteria have actually continued to grow. Studies show that staff adherence to hygiene protocol is appallingly lax. Fortunately, there is a better way to achieve success.

In Search of Positive Deviance

One of the core principles of Positive Deviance is that the community collaborates and searches for sustainable solutions that come from within. The VA Hospital in Pittsburgh decided to apply this principle of Positive Deviance to the problem of lax hygiene.[23] They gathered the entire community of health care workers—doctors, nurses, janitors, kitchen workers, transportation drivers, and pharmacy staff—to give everyone an unprecedented equal voice in solving the problem. When the community is the size of a hospital it's not easy to get everyone involved, so a subset of hospital workers who were the most enthusiastic volunteered to meet daily to look for positive deviance. They interviewed and watched, engaging every level of the organization. One of the hospital pastors realized that the Bible he carried from patient to patient could be a source of infection, so upon his suggestion to the other pastors, they began using disposable book covers and wearing gloves and gowns. Nurses proposed that they all wear personal containers of hand sanitizer when they saw some visitors cleaning their hands that way. And so it continued, with the teams finding workable solutions right in front of them, then educating their peers and embedding new behaviors as the norm. Within one year, hospital-acquired infections at the hospital fell by more than half. Because the behaviors in both Vietnam and the VA Hospital were generated from their respective communities, they were sustainable.

Deficit Mind-Set

We often attack problems from a deficit mind-set, looking for the stickiest, worst parts of the problem and firing at them with all our ammunition. Often outside experts are brought in who point out the flaws in people's thinking, show them how their actions don't measure up, embarrass them, advocate an outsider view as a much better way of doing things, and try to crush resistance. The solutions come in like an invading army, and those inside feel like they have been taken prisoner. Resistance is rampant and as soon as the outsiders leave, everyone goes back to business as usual.

Asset Mind-Set

The asset mind-set looks at difficult situations in a very different way. The approach is to seek out what is going right, no matter how small, and amplify the internal wisdom by giving those people recognition and visibility. In this model, every voice in the community has something to offer; it's a system of inquiry and curiosity, rather than the deficit model of advocacy and mandates. Because ideas are generated from within, from colleagues rather than from outsiders, the community's frame of mind tilts toward acceptance rather than resistance. Behaviors are sustainable because the system already supports the idea in the actions of the positive deviants, and there is no need for buy-in because acceptance is built-in.

Starve Problems and Feed Opportunities

Peter Drucker, the father of management science, encourages the Positive Deviance mind-set in organizations with his suggestion to "starve problems and feed opportunities.[24] The approach has wide application, including to the way we do business. Until her retirement from Hewlett-Packard, Barbara Waugh had the remarkable title of Worldwide Change Manager. She explained in an interview that she would often be introduced as the person in charge of change.[25] "I'm not in charge of anything," she said. "My role is to create mirrors that show the whole what the parts are doing—through coffee talks and small meetings, through building a network, through bringing people together who have similar or complementary ideas." In short, she used her role to amplify the positive deviants throughout the organization.

When she started her career at HP, Barbara was hired to run recruitment. Looking at the demographics, she found that managers were not hiring an equitable number of women and minorities. The excuses were trite and stale; managers said they just could not find enough women and minorities who were qualified engineers and computer scientists. Instead of mandating numbers and getting into a power struggle with those managers, she decided instead to seek positive deviants. Were there any managers at HP who were hiring a reasonable number of women and minorities? She went looking, and found a few. Barbara then focused her attention on these managers. She featured their actions every month in the recruiting newsletter, giving them corporate visibility. She found ways to reward them with time and travel expenses to attend minority recruitment conferences. She lobbied their managers to grant them stock options for their excellent hiring practices, and succeeded. Barbara was effectively rewarding positive deviance and broadcasting it to the entire organization. Everyone else was watching, and within two years Barbara exceeded her goals of hiring and manager transformation.[26]

The benefit of the Positive Deviance approach is that the solution is already in the community and so meets much less resistance than an idea that comes from outside. Change that comes from within—discovered by the community, celebrated by the community, and voluntarily adopted by the people who need to change—is most sustainable.[27]

Expand with "And"

One of the most limiting words that narrows thinking and shrinks possibility is the word OR. Faced with choices, we feel trapped when more than one option has some positive attributes and choosing one option will mean foregoing the attractive parts of the others. We wrestle with the pros and cons of each, trying to decide.

A physicians group in California found themselves in just such a dilemma. Operating medical clinics across the state, they were trying to decide between two new opportunities: opening a clinic either in Palm Springs or Simi Valley. The locations were about a 4-hour drive from each other, serving very different populations. Financially, the medical group only had the resources to open one clinic, so they crunched the numbers to figure out which would be the better choice. Both were good. Frustrated with their inability to find a clear winner, they were ready to toss a coin to pick one and forego the other.

Have you have ever been stuck like this group, trying to decide between options? We often tell the following story to help people expand their scope of possibilities. You will see shortly how it helped the doctors.

The U.S. Constitutional Convention held in 1787 provides a fascinating lesson for resolving dilemmas like the one faced by the medical group. Delegates from the 13 states had convened in Philadelphia to formulate the structure that would become the United States federal government; like many heated negotiations, a debate that threatened to derail the entire process erupted between competing interests. The argument was between small states and large states, and they were at odds about how states should be represented in the government.

Small states like Delaware (population under 40,000) argued that every state had to be equally represented or their voice would never be heard. Large states like Virginia (population over 400,000) argued that equal representation was unfair to their citizens and that states should be represented based on their population. The debate between *equal representation of states* versus *unequal representation of states* became so fierce that many delegates threatened to give up the idea of any federal government at all. How could they possibly choose between these two options? But for James Madison, Benjamin Franklin, and a few others, the purpose of a *United* States of America was so important they were committed to finding a way to expand possibilities with AND. They convened the delegates, telling them that if equal representation was a deal breaker for some of the states, and unequal representation was a deal breaker for other states, they would find a way to do *both*.

After much discussion, these dedicated patriots came up with a groundbreaking plan. They created an innovative system to incorporate both equal *and* unequal representation, devising a form of government with no precedent in history. In the Senate, each state was allotted two senators, giving equal representation to the states. In the House, each state was allotted a number of representatives based on its population, giving the states unequal representation. The division of duties between the Senate and the House was ironed out, the impasse was resolved, and the Constitution was finally ratified.

The medical group used this story to stimulate their thinking. "If it is possible to be both equal and unequal at the same time," they asked themselves, "how can we only open one clinic AND open two clinics at the same time?" It didn't take long for them to realize that they could build a mobile clinic that would spend half the week in Palm Springs and the other half in Simi Valley. It would be enough to establish a client base in each location until resources would allow permanent clinics to be built. They were surprised that they had not thought of this option earlier. However, it is not unusual to see this phenomenon. They had limited their range of thinking with OR, and could not conceive of something better until they expanded their thinking with AND.

In the issues you face, what trade-offs do you typically make? In business projects there may be groups with competing interests; you may also be wrestling with issues of *cost* versus *quality* versus *schedule*. Are there ways in which you could apply AND rather than OR thinking to expand your scope of possibilities?

Small Wins

Albert Einstein said that a problem cannot be solved with the same level of thinking that created it. Large-scale problems cannot be solved with large-scale thinking. When people start thinking about enormous problems, like global hunger, homelessness, or heavy debt, they can seem dauntingly unsolvable; we define the really big problems in ways that overwhelm our ability to think about their entire complexity, and so we do little or nothing.

We've already seen that Positive Deviance is an approach that identifies workable solutions for the seemingly impossible. Another approach, in conjunction with Positive Deviance, is to Think Small.[28] Defining a huge problem as a network of smaller problems means we can work for small wins; we can identify controllable opportunities with manageable scope and shape a success, however small. One small win begets more opportunities, and eventually the many small wins can have a huge impact. For example, in the 1990s violent crime in New York City was eradicated with many small wins, including removing graffiti from subway cars and arrests for public drunkenness and loitering.[29] These small wins might seem unrelated to violent crime, but these wins together with many others sent a message to all criminals that they would no longer be tolerated. In another instance, the Bill & Melinda Gates Foundation is on a mission to provide access to sanitation to the developing world. Almost one out of three people in the world lacks access to even a simple latrine or pit toilet. The lack of sanitation sickens hundreds of millions of people a year. We can decide it's too big to tackle, or it can be approached, as the Gates Foundation has chosen to do, as a network of smaller, winnable problems.[30] The approach of the Gates Foundation is to focus on making a difference within communities rather than wrestling with national governments or trying to solve the problem all at once on a global scale.

Big problems don't have to exist on a massive scale. The U.S. Olympic basketball organizers were overwhelmed in 2004 when the team lost the gold. Coach K, in contrast, approached the building of the 2008 team as a network of small wins. For example, the standard of "no bad practices" meant that in their months of training, every time the team got on the court the practice would be fully scrutinized and problems would be resolved within that session. Tony Hsieh, CEO of online shoe and clothing retailer Zappos, has applied the concept of small wins in the company's career advancement program. Rather than give big promotions every 18 months, employees on the advancement track now get a promotion every 6 months. They have a greater sense of progress and are thus happier, even though it still takes the same three years to finish the program.[31]

Even for the individual, small wins may be the crucial strategy to help tackle major hurdles like debt. Researchers at Northwestern University's Kellogg School of Management found that just getting started and paying off smaller debts first, rather than trying to pay off the largest debt first, made it much more likely that a person would ultimately be successful at paying off their total debts.[32]

Using a Miracle Scale for Personal Goals

Each of us can have personal problems that overwhelm us. Maybe you want to be a confident and articulate public speaker, but that seems unthinkable today, given that just imagining that you might have to speak in front of a group makes your heart race and knees buckle.

(In case that is you, take heart that you are not alone! Surveys show people fear public speaking more than death.) Perhaps you think that becoming a confident public speaker would require nothing less than a miracle. What can we do to make our personal miracle goals more realistically achievable?

Suppose you were to rate yourself on a scale of 0 to 10, where 10 is the achievement of the miracle. In this example, a 10 is the confident and articulate speaker you want to be. You might say that you are a 2, because at least you can speak to people who visit your home. So first of all, congratulations, you are not a 0! But even if you did rate yourself a 0, no matter—you are going to start moving slowly up the miracle scale. If you are a 2, what behaviors would make you a 3? Perhaps speaking up at a team meeting? You might respond, "Oh, no! That's too much!" No problem. You define the behaviors that would make you a 3; nobody else defines them for you. And we're not talking about a 10, just a 3. You might say that striking up a conversation with people who sit at the communal lunch tables in the company cafeteria would be a 3. Great! For the next two weeks, make a point of having some sort of conversation every day at lunch with your tablemates. Start small, just say hello. The point is to take actions that are so small they seem trivial or even silly. In so doing, you will be moving toward your miracle. When we reconvene two weeks later, you have become a 3. Now you will decide what a 4 looks like and then practice those behaviors for a few weeks, until being a 4 feels comfortable.

Nobody can jump from a 2 to a 10, but anyone can take little steps to move up the scale, one notch at a time. Haven't cleaned your cluttered office in years? Start by throwing out one item. Then clean the top right corner of your desk. Then spend exactly 5 minutes a day cleaning what you can and then stop. Want to become a person who exercises 30 minutes a day but you always give up? Start by walking in place during one 30-second commercial while watching TV. Then walk in place during a whole commercial break. Build slowly. Very slowly! You are better off exercising for 30 seconds a day than not exercising for 30 minutes a day. The value of the miracle scale is that you are focusing on smaller wins that feel attainable, not the remote, audacious, heart-stopping, paralyzing end goal that looms too far out in the distant future. You are bringing the future to the present, one step at a time.[33]

How's Life?

Are there any emotions that contribute significantly to our ability to conquer uncertainty and shape success?

Happiness

For too many years psychology focused solely on the dreadful mental and emotional illnesses that devastate lives. Recently, however, the Positive Psychology movement has evolved, founded by pioneers at Ivy League institutions, to study happiness. News about happiness research made national headlines when one of the founding researchers offered a course to undergraduates at Harvard, and it became the most popular course ever offered at the university. People took notice; if Harvard undergrads were flocking to a rigorous academic course called "Happiness," what were we missing?! It turns out that happiness, a subjective state of well-being, is the most important emotional element in determining and shaping success. In Chapter 2, "Connect to a Compelling Purpose," we described the three routes that lead to different levels of happiness—the pleasant life, the good life, and the meaningful life—and it is the integration of all three that leads to the greatest life satisfaction and the greatest levels of resilience.[34]

Many companies have taken notice, too. Google is famous for break rooms filled with toys, free gourmet-catered lunches, and "20% Time," during which employees get to spend 20 percent of their time working on a project based on whatever they are passionate about. The Boston Beer Company holds frequent parties at Sammy's Place, the beer bar in the lobby of its headquarters. Netflix has a "no limit" vacation policy, which means people can take as much vacation time as they want as long as they get their jobs done. TripAdvisor allows employees to rotate through teams and departments until they find the best possible fit, and offers pet insurance and adoption assistance to those who need it. Patagonia, the sportswear company, offers a "Let My People Go Surfing" policy with surfboards available in the office should anyone need to hit the waves. Zappos has baked happiness into the culture; CEO Tony Hsieh says that work–life *balance* is a mistake. We have to create work–life *integration*, combining profits, purpose, and passion. "Delivering Happiness" is the stated mission of Zappos.[35] All of these companies and many others have seen increased employee satisfaction lead to greater company success.

What if you don't have surfboards, unlimited vacation time, or beer bars? Improving the subjective well-being of a team can be shockingly simple. Frequent recognition and encouragement is the best tactic used by effective leaders everywhere. It works in corporate settings, non-profits that rely on volunteer commitment, and even the military. U.S. Navy Captain Michael Abrashoff took command of the unhappy crew of the USS *Benfold*, the worst-performing ship in the fleet, and transformed them into a model of collaboration and performance. Before, sailors couldn't leave the ship fast enough and few thought that life on the ship could improve. Under Abrashoff, sailors from other ships clamored to join its crew, and the *Benfold* became the pride of the U.S. Pacific Fleet. The transformation was possible because Abrashoff rejected the traditional, 225-year-old Navy system of command and control. Instead, he vowed to treat every encounter with every sailor as the most important thing in that moment and to really listen. In his first few weeks on the ship, Abrashoff met with each sailor individually to get to know them as people, encouraged them to offer ideas to improve the ship, and then acted on their suggestions. The core of his approach was to engage the hearts as well as the minds of his crew by treating every single person with dignity.[36]

The Motivational Paycheck

Tackling difficult problems to achieve a meaningful purpose is going to require hard work. People are going to get frustrated and discouraged when progress doesn't seem obvious, or when there are setbacks. We like to feel appreciated and valued for our efforts, whether those efforts result in success or not, but recognition is even more important to offset frustration when the results are not what we hoped for. Staying motivated when the going gets tough requires a strong emotional bank account from which we can make withdrawals, and the best deposits into that type of account come from recognition and appreciation.

There are two kinds of recognition systems: formal and informal. Formal systems include awards, certificates, pins, recognition dinners, or events to honor achievements. A monetary bonus is also a formal recognition, and in most organizations, formal recognition is meted out infrequently, maybe just once a year.

To enrich the emotional bank account, however, the most effective recognition occurs in the day-to-day exchanges between team members, through simple acts that demonstrate sincere appreciation for the efforts team members bring to the group. Celebrating people on a team should start early. When Iris's youngest daughter got her first corporate job after college graduation, she was joining a team of eight people. On her first day at work, the manager took the whole team out to lunch to celebrate her arrival, and when they got back to the office her work area was decorated with balloons and banners to welcome her. Imagine her immediate sense of belonging. In the all-too-typical organization, such celebrations are reserved for retirement parties!

There are many ways for us to celebrate one another. Informal recognition is most appreciated, and best improves morale and performance, when it is *timely*, *personally relevant*, *novel*, *simple*, *appropriate*, and *consistent*.

Timely means it happens when it is still pertinent. If someone puts in great effort over a weekend, the celebration of their effort should happen Monday morning, not six weeks later or at the end of the project.

Personally relevant means it is meaningful to the recipient, demonstrating individual attention. Don't bring someone a gift card to Starbucks if they never drink coffee. When a reward doesn't fit the person, it doesn't work. If a reward is generic, it also has less impact. Don't assume that others appreciate the same things you do. Learn more about people to know what they uniquely care about.

Novel means that variety and the unexpected nature of the act add to its value. Our brains are attuned to novelty; we habituate to the same stimulus repeated over and over, and the reward loses its impact. Even if your team member loves Starbucks, after the sixth coffee gift card in a row it's no longer novel and becomes much less meaningful. Use a variety of methods so celebrations don't get predictable and stale; leverage the element of surprise.

Simple means that the efforts we are recognizing are the little things that add up, so the form of recognition should match in kind. When someone volunteers to cover for a teammate who is out sick, or someone stays late to help meet a deadline, a reward that is out of proportion or overly effusive can even be insulting.

Appropriate means that the recognition is socially acceptable. Imagine that you invite friends to dinner in your home, you have spent the day cooking, and at the end of the meal, one of your friends pulls out $10 and puts it on the table as a tip. You would be shocked! If another friend sent flowers to thank you, however, you would be delighted. As obvious as this may seem, misunderstandings abound, especially if there are cultural differences. In China, the colors black, white, and blue, and four of anything, are negatively associated with death. Sharp objects like a knife represent the severing of a relationship—including a business relationship. Red is a lucky color in China, but in Japan it means death—so be careful about the color of ink you use if you write a card! When in doubt, ask others if your idea is appropriate.

Consistent means celebrate one another often. Recognition and praise have a short shelf life; they wear off quickly, and people need a lot more than they typically get. One of the most pervasive complaints on teams is that people don't feel appreciated often enough, while those in charge feel that they are constantly showing appreciation.

How Much Recognition Is Enough?

Life is attended by positive as well as negative experiences. Negative experiences are etched more indelibly in memory than positive ones. Negative emotions are felt more deeply and persist for a longer period of time than do positive emotions. Therefore, to reach emotional equilibrium, we need to balance the negative with more frequent and more abundant positive experiences.

Marcial Losada, a psychologist, has studied happiness and found that successful teams experience three-fold more positive interactions than negative interactions in the workplace. By this, Losada means that it takes about three positive experiences (e.g., compliments and other forms of recognition), to mitigate the effect of one negative experience. Although some may argue the validity of the exact ratio between the positive and the negative, the fact remains that the higher the ratio, the more effective the team.

You might reasonably think that exceptionally successful teams have lots to be positive about and that is why their ratio is high; that success leads to the higher number of positive interactions relative to negative ones. While this can be true, Losada has shown that by changing the ratio, underperforming teams can turn around and become successful. He worked with a mining company suffering production losses of more than 10 percent and found that their ratio between positive and negative was close to 1. After team leaders started to use recognition and encouragement the average team ratio exceeded 3 and led to production gains of over 40 percent.[37]

Get creative and list ways to provide recognition. Here is a list to get started.

1. Say "thank you"—often!
2. Bring them coffee
3. Fix something for them
4. Ask their opinion
5. Compliment them
6. Greet them with a smile and positive comment
7. Brag about them in their presence
8. Write a thank-you note—on paper, in a card, or in an e-mail
9. Show interest in their lives
10. Bring them a newspaper article you think they will find interesting
11. Give them something you know their kids will like because you have taken an interest in their family
12. Put up a banner or sign outside their office
13. Acknowledge them when you see them (and introduce them if you are talking to someone else)
14. And one more time: Say "thank you"—often!

Celebrate People and Process, Not Just Outcome

A subtle but crucial point is to say "thank you" in a meaningful way, emphasizing the behaviors and standards, not just the outcome. Suppose a team is working to create a new software program and the beta testing is showing promise. Don't say, "Congratulations, the software is looking good!" Better to say, "Congratulations! Because of your dedicated efforts, team spirit, and creative thinking, the software is looking good!" Recognize and celebrate behaviors that colleagues can control and repeat. Even when an outcome is less than anticipated, living up to standards ought to be acknowledged.

When someone shares good news with us, the best response offers enthusiastic support, specific comments, and follow-up interest ("That's great! I'm glad to hear your long weekends and creative negotiation strategy had such an impact! When does the partnership start?"). In contrast, other responses are relationship crushers. General responses ("How nice.") can be as destructive to the relationship as overtly insulting responses ("You?! You've never been able to pull off a contract before!"). Ignoring the news altogether is yet another way to damage the relationship ("OK, yeah, well. . . . remind me again, what time is the conference call this afternoon?"), as is no response at all.[38]

What Good Is All This Positivity?

Beyond just feeling good, positive emotions alter mind-sets and change the brain in beneficial, long-lasting ways. Barbara Fredrickson has shown that negative emotions limit thinking to a narrow repertoire of possibility, whereas positive emotions broaden accessibility to a wider range of thoughts and actions than is the norm.[39] Decades of studies have shown that people experiencing positive emotions show patterns of thought that are more creative, flexible, inclusive, open to new ideas, and efficient; they cope more effectively with chronic stress, are better able to step back from problems and see the big picture, and discover better solutions in negotiations. In addition, positive emotion enhances ability to cope with negative events or unpleasant information; people are less defensive and can better focus on relevant negative information that they need to know. Negative emotions shrink these same capacities.[40]

Even moderate shifts in positive feelings can systematically affect thinking. Mild positive emotions, like amusement and cheer, improve creative problem-solving, recall, and decision-making strategies. Positive feelings lead to cognitive flexibility, which leads to more thoughts, more atypical thoughts, and innovative solutions to problems. These findings have been tested and found in real-world settings such as consumer choices, team negotiations, and physicians diagnosing disease. And even though positive emotions are short lived, the changes they produce in thoughts, actions, and even physiological responses have long-term consequences.[41]

Emotions in the Brain

Brain researchers are studying how positive emotions physically change the brain. Recent findings tell us that these emotions not only change the brain while we are experiencing the emotion, but also change the brain for extended periods thereafter. We can get a lot of mileage out of brief but frequent spurts of positive emotion.[42]

Emotions play out in the brain in an intricate choreography among various brain structures and their interaction with the neurotransmitter dopamine, which responds to pleasure. The prefrontal cortex, the part of your brain just behind your forehead, is the area used for judgment, planning, and decision making—and is particularly influenced by the type of emotion being experienced. Positive emotional states shift the level of electrical activity in the left side of the prefrontal cortex. Greater left-side activation is associated with increased ability to bounce back from a disappointment, greater tendency to lean in to a challenge (rather than to back away), greater ability to engage in abstract thinking, greater capacity to extract general rules from concrete situations, and enhanced working memory—exactly the kind of skills needed to conquer uncertainty.[43] (If you're going to get hit in the head, make sure it's not on the left side!)Dopamine further enables effective thinking because it has a calming impact on the amygdala, the part of the brain that processes fear and anxiety, and quiets down activity there.[44]

Dopamine also affects the parts of the brain that help you reevaluate the relative importance of factors in a decision. For example, if you were planning with a friend to meet for coffee on Friday, and you were trying to work around the various appointments you have, if your friend suggested finding a time on Saturday instead, you would have to be able to mentally shift away and stop factoring your Friday appointments into the decision since they are no longer relevant. There are parts of the brain dedicated to this ability, and they, too, function better with dopamine.[45]

Three Cheers for Dopamine!

Another interesting dopamine pathway in the brain that is highly active during positive emotion influences motor activity. We've all experienced intense happiness that makes us "jump for joy." We literally cannot sit still. An Olympic runner who has just won a gold medal has to run another lap around the track, arms stretched out. Even sitting in our chairs, we raise our arms and pump the air after hearing good news.

It turns out that dopamine response is most intense in the presence of an unanticipated reward. After a reward becomes routine or expected, dopamine-cell firing is greatly reduced. Dopamine cells fire in the presence of an unanticipated reward for only a few seconds, but the chemical itself stays in our system for at least 30 minutes after the cells have stopped firing, which is why we continue to feel good. Somebody walks by the office, gives us a high five, and says "Good job!" It bathes our brain in dopamine, we continue to bask in the pleasure of the compliment long after they are gone, and our brains thrive.

Celebrate, Encourage, and Prime to Shape Success

Going back to the beginning of this chapter, emotional engagement is essential for the focus and perseverance needed to achieve extraordinary outcomes. The daily huddle primes us to look for standards and notice the positive deviants who already are acting on the standards, even in small ways. Use the huddle to celebrate the small wins. Repeating the mind-set daily turns it into a habit that soon becomes second nature. It becomes easier to find new ways to live up to the standards. At the same time, make a special effort to inject positive surprise and novelty wherever possible. Keep it fresh. These celebrations and other moments of encouragement increase team well-being and motivate healthier brains that are better equipped to successfully conquer uncertainty and shape the future.

■ ■ ■

In pursuit of purpose, conquering the uncertainty of the future is a challenge for everyone. In the next chapter, we explore the powerful strategy of "bringing the future to the present," in our quest to eliminate uncertainty where possible, reduce uncertainty where we can, and embrace it as needed to thrive and succeed.

5

CONQUER UNCERTAINTY

Bring the Future to the Present

FOR AS LONG AS THE HUMAN BRAIN HAS BEEN ABLE TO IMAGINE THE FUTURE, we have been trying to make uncertain events more predictable. Whether through prophets, tea leaves, mathematical models, or empirical studies of cause and effect, people have searched for tools to help reduce the uncertainty of the future. During the scientific revolution that started in the 1500s, people thought that models could be developed that would allow them to finally dispel all doubt about the future. All they had to do was find the initial conditions that started the universe, plug those conditions into sophisticated equations, and they would be able to predict any event—past, present, and future. This belief was reinforced in the late 1600s by the success of Isaac Newton's theory that described the motion of planets around the sun. Astonishingly for the time, Newton's model made it possible to predict future eclipses of the sun and moon, the tides of the oceans, and even the existence and location of planets that had not yet been discovered—but that were soon confirmed by observation. Newton and other thought leaders of his day had come to believe that the universe was orderly, knowable, and ultimately predictable.

Because of his reputation and stature in Britain as an eminent scientist, in 1699 Isaac Newton was appointed master of the British Royal Mint. Newton took his new job seriously, and applied his scientific thinking to money,[1] creating the concept of the gold standard in 1717. The gold standard created a stable and predictable value for currency because money would now only be printed based on a rule of equivalence with gold. For every ounce of gold excavated from mines, the British government would have the authority to print a corresponding value represented in paper money. The gold standard was subsequently embraced by countries all over the world, allowing for greater predictability—and less uncertainty—over the value of paper notes globally.

During this same time, a group of British business speculators had formed the South Sea Company, with exclusive rights to trade with Latin American colonies owned by Spain. Within six months of issuance, the stock value of the company had increased 800 percent and continued to soar upwards. One of the investors in the stock was our very same Isaac Newton. When the unexpected happened and the bubble inevitably burst, South Sea stock collapsed; Newton's loss exceeded 20,000 pounds sterling, the equivalent of 40 years of his salary. Devastated and chastened, he lamented later, "I can calculate the movement of the stars, but not the madness of men."

The same Newton who was so rigorous in his thinking with his models of planets, so visionary that as master of the British Royal Mint he devised a system to anchor the printing of money, was blinded by uncertainty and made personal investments with an inherently flawed model because it ignored the possibility that the value of the South Sea Company could collapse. Newton had been swept up by the same surge of emotion that guides many of us to follow mass action without giving any regard to the uncertainties of the future.

Newton was a brilliant scientist, and he had applied his thinking to two fundamentally different types of problems that, unfortunately for Newton, cannot be approached the same way. The problem of understanding the movement of the planets was a *complicated system* to unravel. The problem of economics and investments, by contrast, is a *complex system* to understand. What is the difference?

Complicated Systems and Complex Systems

Let's look at an example. The engineering of a modern commercial airplane is a complicated system. There are buttons and levers in the cockpit, and many of these are connected and work interdependently to control other parts of the plane. Engineers working with aviation experts are able to calculate the risk of any set of parts not working—the probability that they will fail and the potential impact on the ability of the plane to still fly. They can therefore create increasingly better backup systems for redundancy to make the risk of catastrophe due to failing parts close to zero. Once engineers know how to build one plane, the same algorithms can be used to successfully build additional planes, or take a plane apart and reassemble it, without changing any of the original design. The whole of the airplane is the sum of its parts. The factors impacting the success of a complicated system are knowable.

An example of a complex system is air traffic control. Air traffic controllers have to react to weather changes, plane delays, and airport problems. They are thus constantly adjusting as situations unfold, and there is always uncertainty about the next set of conditions they will have to manage. Included in the uncertainty are two kinds of events: random variations and outlier events. Random variation is the easier kind to manage; for example, they know that weather can range in severity and air turbulence has to be assessed accordingly, so they monitor it on an ongoing basis and adjust flight plans in real time. The outlier events are the ones that can create disruptive, chaotic disturbance to the system itself. For example, when the terrorist attacks of 9/11 hit the United States, it was unknown whether more attacks were imminent, so the directive was given to land every plane still in the air immediately. Air traffic controllers had never considered the possibility of national attack using airplanes, so there was no contingency plan for such a possibility; nevertheless, they had to land every plane in the country within the hour. The air traffic control system had to adapt itself in real time. Complex systems can adapt to situations that are not foreseen in advance.

Complex systems differ from complicated systems because they have to account for the kind of uncertainties that are not just random variations, but rather the emergence of events that are not within the known scope of possibilities. The system is in constant flux and the parts—especially when those parts are people—are changing as they adapt to changes happening to and within the system. Any time people and their behaviors are part of a system, we are in the domain of the complex.[2] To paraphrase Newton, we can calculate the movement of the stars as part of a complicated system, but not the infinite possible actions of people as part of a complex system.

Perils of Ignoring Uncertainty

When we approach complex systems with tools and algorithms designed for complicated systems, we ignore uncertainty and invite calamity. Let us fast-forward a few hundred years from Newton's unfortunate investments, to 1993. A firm is established with the promising name of Long Term Capital Management (LTCM). Among the founders were two brilliant economists, Robert Merton and Myron

Scholes. The model LTCM used was an appealingly short mathematical equation that would guide their investment strategy. Clients attracted to LTCM had to invest a minimum of $10 million, and included many large banks. The initial success of the company was spectacular. Within four years investors saw their money quadruple. The founders were so confident that nothing could go wrong that they decided to return money to clients and instead borrow funds from banks themselves so that they would not have to share the enormous profits with outsiders. In October 1997, Merton and Scholes were awarded the Nobel Prize in Economics. But the future was about to come crashing in and send them into a tailspin. In 1998, the Russian financial system collapsed and the government defaulted on its debt, which came in the wake of the Southeast Asian monetary crisis just a few months earlier. The effect was contagious, and stock markets imploded worldwide. LTCM's asset values and profits evaporated. "Long" Term Capital Management did not survive a term of even four years.[3]

What went wrong? While LTCM claimed to have a model that conquered risk, they had ignored uncertainty. A model is inherently a simplification, and by design it leaves out some of the variables, as well as factors that we don't even know that we don't know—that is, uncertainty. The crisis that caused the demise of the meteorically successful company within four years was defined by one of the firm's founders as "a ten sigma event"—so improbable that it would happen no more than once in the history of the universe. But probability and possibility are two different things.

"Satisfice" versus "Optimize"

Both Newton and LTCM were tightly aligned with classical economic theory, which assumes that people are rational beings whose goal is to maximize expected value and optimize choice. In essence, the behavior of people was thought of no differently than the movement of the planets, with predictable rules that guided action. However, in 1978, Herbert Simon received the Nobel Prize in Economics for demonstrating that people often "satisfice" rather than optimize choice. Namely, we often pick an alternative that is good enough rather than perfect. "Good enough" means that human judgment and quirks of individual perceptions of value are part of the choice process. In 2002,

Daniel Kahneman was awarded the Nobel Prize in Economics for his research with the late Amos Tversky. Their work revealed that as we assess which alternatives are good enough, we take cognitive short cuts to save time and mental energy, and in doing so, we express biases in thinking.

The relatively new fields of behavioral finance and behavioral economics, founded on the work of Kahneman and Tversky, are predicated on the fact that finance and economics are not divorced from the vagaries and uncertainties of human behavior. Thus we cyclically end up with bubbles, the result of the inherently human tendency to believe in an optimistic future and take mental short cuts while ignoring or discounting uncertainties. Newton found himself the victim of the South Seas bubble, even though less than 100 years earlier Dutch investors had found themselves caught in a tulip bubble (people invested the equivalent of a year's salary for a single tulip bulb!). Americans in the 1990s experienced a dot-com bubble, but optimistically believed that the same could never happen with housing . . . and then, barely a decade later, the housing bubble burst. Even as we write, another bubble is almost certainly forming somewhere.

Information and Uncertainty

In the twenty-first century, global uncertainty has increased, which is ironic in a world in which we have access to much more information than ever before. The information explosion and our instant-communication tools have helped lessen local uncertainty, but those same links have heightened global uncertainty. For example, we use GPS to find where traffic is building so we don't have to guess what route to take, and we use the Internet to monitor the interest rates of banks and stock prices to know the value of our investments at any moment in time. However, because everyone on the planet can be linked to the same websites, they too can act on the same information, and this is how exposure to information can create magnified uncertainties. If everyone knows which roads are open, suddenly those routes may become jammed. A local blip of financial activity can cascade into an international crash. Because of our interconnected world, global meltdowns that were few and far between are now regular occurrences with increasing frequency.

The question, then, is how to deal with complex systems that by definition include the uncertainty of the unknown. We need a different way of thinking, one that puts us in a state of readiness to adapt and respond effectively to whatever the future holds. In the rest of this chapter, we will discuss how to bring the future to the present to adapt in ways that help us conquer uncertainty. To conquer uncertainty means that we eliminate it wherever possible, reduce it when we can, and embrace it strategically everywhere else.

Bring the Future to the Present

The deeper we peer into the future, the more uncertainty there is. So how can you possibly strategize and plan for a future rife with unknowns? Imagine if it were possible to somehow wrap your arms around the future and bring it to the present. You would have a much better picture and a lot less uncertainty. While this may sound like it requires impossible time travel or heroic superpowers, in fact it is possible to mitigate uncertainty with thinking strategies that use the power of the human mind. The next few sections describe several ways to bring the future to the present to conquer uncertainty.

Create Clear Pictures of the Future

In 1501, the artist Michelangelo was awarded the opportunity to carve the statue of David from a flawed block of marble. When he was asked how he had created the figure, he allegedly replied, "I looked at the slab of marble and chiseled away everything that was not David." Almost 500 years later, Nelson Mandela was elected in a historic referendum to carve a new South Africa, shaping a dramatically different country that he had envisioned from his prison cell, a country that would embrace reconciliation between the races, create room for the aspirations of all its citizens, and become a beacon of hope to all.

How were Michelangelo and Mandela able to see future possibilities that others did not? How does anyone develop the ability to clearly envision the future? We can harness the power of imagination to create clearer and more vivid pictures of the future to shape better outcomes.

Stories Engage the Whole Brain

The speech that Martin Luther King, Jr., delivered on the steps of the Lincoln Memorial on August 28, 1963, is forever seared in the collective memory of Americans because he painted a vivid and compelling picture for us of what we could be. In his message he told us that as a country, we had set standards for ourselves and we were not living up to them:

> . . . I have a dream that one day this nation will rise up and live out the true meaning of its creed: "We hold these truths to be self-evident, that all men are created equal."

Instead of providing data and statistics on racial inequality in the present, he painted a picture of possibility for the future, of what we could become:

> . . . that one day on the red hills of Georgia sons of former slaves and the sons of former slave-owners will be able to sit down together at the table of brotherhood. I have a dream that one day even the state of Mississippi, a state sweltering with the heat of injustice, sweltering with the heat of oppression, will be transformed into an oasis of freedom and justice.
>
> I have a dream that my four little children will one day live in a nation where they will not be judged by the color of their skin but by the content of their character. I have a dream today.

Everyone knew that racial inequalities existed, but it was King's vivid verbal images that connected with us emotionally and propelled the federal government to take legislative action, resulting in the Civil Rights Act of 1964 and the Voting Rights Act of 1965.

Humans have been telling stories with pictures for 100,000 years and with language for over 10,000 years. Our brains are innately wired to respond to stories and transport us into the narrative. Stories are the equivalent of our species' native language. It takes years for the brain to develop the capacity to think with numbers—just try to give a Power-Point presentation with data to a two-year-old. But tell them a story and they are transfixed. As adults, our brains can process raw data, but it requires more cognitive effort than listening to a story. With a compelling story, we are all transported into worlds of other possibilities, activating the powers of imagination. We agree with Albert Einstein, who said, "Imagination is more important than knowledge. For knowledge is limited to all we now know and understand, while imagination embraces the entire world, and all there ever will be to know and understand."

Telling a provocative story, with judicious use of descriptive data wrapped within the story, has a much greater impact on shaping the future than the mind-numbing data dump all too typical in business meetings. Cognitive psychologists have repeatedly shown that facts embedded in the context of a story are much more memorable than isolated facts presented as a list.[4] Stories engage many more parts of the brain than facts presented like a barrage of bullets (or PowerPoint bullet points).

Stories are the way to move people, to change how they feel so they will change how they act. To motivate action, people have to care. Neuroscientists have shown that our decisions are driven by emotional responses even when we are unaware of it. In fact, without engaging the emotional part of our brains, we would be unable to make any decisions at all. This discovery was dramatically demonstrated by the neuroscientist Antonio Damasio as he was working with a patient, Eliot, whose emotional center of his brain was damaged.[5] Eliot was highly intelligent, and even after the brain damage his IQ was in the top 3 percent. However, because he had lost the ability to feel emotion, Eliot would deliberate endlessly over irrelevant details, like which chair to sit in, or whether to use a black or blue pen to write a note. Other patients with such damage exhibit a similar inability to judge when something is good, bad, or irrelevant. Free of emotion and faced with choice, there is no internal thermometer telling them, "That doesn't matter!" Subjecting every choice to pro and con analysis, there is never an obvious "best."

For the fully intact brain, emotion and reason together choreograph choice; we may coolly rationalize decisions with logic and data, but the context of the decision is understood by the emotional part of the brain, motivating us to take action. It would be impossible for us to satisfice (choose a solution that is good enough) or even compromise with others in the absence of emotion. Instead, we would endlessly try to optimize every decision. Emotion is at the core of simplification and redeems us from an unyielding dependence on certainty. Stories engage this more fully connected brain.[6]

Emotion Trumps Logic

The rational mind makes New Year resolutions; I, Iris, vow to eat fruit instead of cake for dessert for the next 12 months. The rational brain knows that the fruit is healthier, but two weeks later at a party, faced with fruit and cake, I *know* I should eat the fruit, but I *feel* like eating the cake! In the tug-of-war between the two parts of the brain, feeling trumps reasoning more often than not. To override my desire to eat the cake, I have to make it emotionally undesirable rather than logically undesirable. If I try to reason with myself and say that the indulgence is not worth the extra calories, another voice in my head can counter the argument and say that I will only have this one piece of cake and eat fruit the rest of the week. Instead, I have to engage the emotional brain, so I tell myself a story; I imagine that just before I got to the buffet table, someone sneezed all over the cake. I create a disgustingly clear picture of the result, and all desire for the cake evaporates.

How, then, did I turn attraction into aversion? I made a rational decision to engage the emotional brain, and used the stronger negative emotion of disgust to neutralize the emotion of desire. Logic does not trump emotion, but one emotion can trump another.

Pictures of the Distant Future

Many organizations are recognizing the power of stories to create clear pictures and motivate action to shape the more distant future. General Electric is a global company whose goal is to make their own products obsolete before somebody else does it to them. They e-publish GE Reports, with stories about the very tough challenges they seek to solve. German engineering and electronics giant Siemens looks 10 to 20 years into the future and publishes a *Pictures of the Future* e-magazine twice a year, envisioning synergies between technologies and business. The front page is all pictures, and clicking on an icon brings the reader into a story about the future that Siemens aspires to invent.[7]

An exercise we often use with teams is using story to imagine their future. We ask the group to imagine that, five years from now, the *Wall Street Journal* has written about their team in a front-page article. The group then collaborates to write the article—what did they accomplish that warranted publication in a national newspaper? With our guidance, we ask them to take a mental leap into the future, and to write the article in the past tense as though their achievements have already been realized. We instruct them to dream big and generate as much detail as possible around *what* was achieved. Once the article is finalized, the team comes back to the present and must begin thinking about *how* they achieved this vivid future state.

Pictures of the Immediate Future

There are organizations that have already found ways to create better pictures, especially of the immediate future, to reduce or eliminate uncertainty. Many cities have smartphone applications that let commuters know exactly when the next bus or train will arrive at the station; no standing around wondering how much longer you will have to wait. Package delivery companies like FedEx have tracking systems that allow us to follow the path of our mail and know both where it is at any given time, and when to expect its arrival. On the Domino's website you can even track your pizza order, following your food from the moment it's prepared to the moment it leaves the store. Even without technology, there are ways to reduce the uncertainty of the immediate future. As you progress through a line at a theme park, signs indicate how much longer the wait will be at incremental milestones along the way. At the airport and bank, a single line feeding into multiple agents' stations does not indicate how long it will take, but at least eliminates the frustration of trying to guess which line will move fastest. A terrific picture of the immediate future is provided to drivers entering the parking lots of Westfield shopping centers. Many of their parking lots now have sensors in each parking space. A light bulb above each spot shines either red, if the spot is occupied, or green, if it is available. Instead of inching through the lot looking for an open spot, with a quick scan of the whole ceiling drivers see where available spots are. Information that used to be hidden is now accessible to those who need it.

Perceptions

In a world of complexity, one of the ways we reduce uncertainty is to learn from others. In the past, we were only able to communicate with and tap into the experiences of people within our geographically accessible community. In fact, the words *community* and *communication* are derived from the same root. The old definition of *community* was the distance a communication could travel within 24 hours. For example, in the days of limited transportation, imagine walking or getting on your horse; how far could you get in 24 hours? That was the size of your community. Your communications were with very few people, and typically these were people who were very similar to you in terms of background and experiences. They knew what you knew.

Applying the same definition today—the distance a communication can travel in 24 hours—what defines your community? Endlessly large, broadly diverse, and instantaneously accessible.

Suppose you want to buy a set of fancy dishes but you are uncertain whether their gold trim, which looks so elegant in the store, will hold up as they go through the dishwasher. Today, you can check out the consumer reviews posted by people who may live thousands of miles away who have already purchased those dishes. Your potential future using the dishes is already their past experience. If review after review says the dishes chip, you have conquered your uncertainty. Millions of people a month visit Yelp.com for user reviews, people planning trips log in to TripAdvisor.com to learn from others who have already travelled to those locations, and before clicking Buy Now, Amazon.com customers can see what other readers thought about a book. The Internet has amplified the power of others to help us reduce uncertainty.

Marketers understand how wired we are to learn from others to reduce our own uncertainty; even before the Internet, Ray Kroc tapped into the power of the perceptions of others in 1955, when he hung the sign declaring "Over 1 Million Served" next to the first McDonald's. In our mind, the aggregate of all these diverse and independent users is the same pattern identified millions of times over by different brains. If so many others, unrelated to one another, have already gone through the experience and have come to similar conclusions, we become more confident that we know what the future holds for us if we embark on this experience. While it is not a foolproof rule because the whole world can also be wrong, on the whole it is a very useful heuristic.

Reducing the uncertainty of the future by tapping into other people's past and present experiences is one way to bring the future to the present. Your potential future has already been experienced by others. Building on this, we can also use the power of the perceptions of others to reduce the uncertainty of futures none of us has yet fully experienced.

Together We're a Genius

Imagine you are on the eighteenth floor of a high-rise building, looking out a window facing east. If you only look out through that one window and describe what you see, you know that the view will be different from the other directions, from other windows that provide another frame of reference. In the physical world it's easy enough to walk over to another window and get another view. In the cognitive world, the most effective way to get those other views is through other people. Imagine that in the high-rise building there are other people with you, each standing at a different window, on a different floor. You see busy city streets and many other high-rise buildings. From another direction, someone says that they see a river and a large park. Down on the third floor someone tells you they see a small dog in the park. Would you tell them that this is impossible because you don't see it from your window? Hardly; you know the physical views and level of observable detail can be different from the different floors and directions. Yet, when we have conversations with people who have different world views, we often reject their ideas because that's not how we see those issues through our frame of reference.

What Were They Thinking?!

We have seen how even geniuses like Isaac Newton, and Nobel Prize winners like Merton and Scholes, are not immune to miscalculating the impact of uncertainty. Jason Zweig, in his book *Your Money and Your Brain*, tells the story of Harvard philosopher Willard Van Orman Quine, who, as a young scholar, took the question mark key off his typewriter. Managing to type for 70 years without a question mark, he explained that he did not need one.[8]

There are endless examples of people and organizations that assume the way they see the world is reliably how everyone else will see things, when instead the rest of us ask, "What were they thinking?!" In a world of uncertainty, we need to add extra question marks to our mental keyboards, asking more questions from divergent thinkers before choosing solutions, instead of assuming that everyone perceives and thinks just like us and we can know exactly how the future will unfold using only our own perspective.

David Gergen, former advisor to four presidents, tells of the time Richard Nixon visited Charles de Gaulle in France and, impressed by the regal uniforms worn by the French palace guards, ordered them for the White House security staff. The first day the staff wore them in Washington, reporters laughed so hard that Nixon was immediately forced to backtrack, and the ridiculous uniforms were donated to a college marching band.[9]

Entire organizations can get caught in the trap of a limited perspective. When Bank of America announced in 2011 that it would start charging $5 per month for debit card usage, clients were so outraged that even after the bank cancelled the planned fee, customers closed their accounts in protest.[10] Also in 2011, Netflix announced a plan to split into two services (Netflix for streaming and Qwikster for discs in the mail). Public outcry was so fierce that Netflix backed away from their plan, which would have complicated movie orders.[11]

Organizations like Bank of America and Netflix can misperceive what people will think, and they are often genuinely surprised by the reaction of customers. As an another example, in 2009 Dell unveiled "Della," a new site with computers targeted to women. Produced in a variety of pastel colors, Della included software for fashion videos, dieting tips, recipes, calorie counters, and other cutesy applications that infuriated and offended women, who called the offering demeaning, condescending, and sexist. After a few days of relentless criticism, Dell realized that they had erred; they had no choice but to respond to the huge backlash, and on their website declared, "You spoke; we listened."[12]

What could Dell have done differently? For that matter, what could Richard Nixon, Bank of America, and Netflix have done to avoid the respective embarrassment, wrath, and wasted investment they incurred? Engaging the perceptions of others before embarking on a path might have prompted insights that could have prevented the debacles. We call this a system of creating *deliberate chaos* very early in the thinking process.

Deliberate Chaos

Aggregating multiple, diverse perceptions in the very early stages of thinking creates deliberate chaos. It is similar to a jigsaw puzzle, with each cardboard puzzle piece representing a viewpoint, question, possibility, data point, or fact in the conversation. Imagine throwing all the pieces of a 5,000-piece puzzle on the floor. Now imagine taking 500 pieces from another, unrelated puzzle, and mixing them into the mess. You have no idea how the pieces will fit together, and you don't know which pieces are irrelevant. A similar thing happens cognitively when we bring multiple perceptions into a conversation. It is not clear how any of them will ultimately fit together, and we don't initially know what's relevant and what we can safely ignore. Given the effort required to create deliberate chaos in the early stages of thinking, there had better be good reason to do it. In fact, there are several good reasons, not the least of which is the social capital you build with the early inclusion of all stakeholders.[13]

Benefits of Deliberate Chaos

One of the great powers of the human mind is the ability to create structure and coherence, and to find patterns in widely disparate cues. Tapping into brains that are wired to see the world differently, deliberate chaos makes us more likely to start with more of the important cues, more likely to identify novel and innovative patterns, and more likely to devise responses that will create value into the future. Unfortunately, under time and resource constraints, we too often rush through the process; we only see the cues most obvious to our frame of reference and assume the future will be more of the same. We thus make inferences to fill in perceptual gaps, and identify a pattern that more or less fits in order to quickly devise a response and take action. When the outcomes disappoint, and errors have to be rectified, this is the emergent chaos so common in organizations. Richard Nixon, Bank of America, Netflix, and Dell experienced emergent chaos because they did not start with the deliberate chaos that mitigates uncertainty.

Deliberate Chaos Enhances Early Error Detection

When we engage with others as we think about and plan for the future, they may know of or detect potential problems and pitfalls outside our scope of awareness. The frame of reference and knowledge that others bring to the conversation can inform our thinking, instead of letting us bumble down a path only to discover, too late, that there were minefields ahead. There is no end to the errors that result from not having information that we could have known had we asked the right questions. Catching errors before they become a crisis can save money, time, and reputation. When an error is caught very early, before plans have been formulated, steps can be taken to prevent the problem altogether. When we are already starting to devise potential responses, we might detect errors that we call an *early catch*; steps may have to be taken to mitigate the error, but they require minimal resources. Errors that we catch after resources have been allocated and we are set to execute a plan are now *near-misses*; we sense that we were close to disaster, but we saved the situation in the nick of time. The cost to correct them is already greater but crisis has been averted. If an error survives into the execution of the response, we now have a problem to *solve*. The more errors we catch early, the fewer problems there are to solve when the cost in money, time, or reputation can be prohibitive.

Deliberate Chaos Reduces Aversion to Revision

The mental traps of sunk costs, loss aversion, and risk aversion often impel us to stick with paths of action that are not in our best interest. Deliberate chaos helps to create better options early, before we commit to ideas that will be more difficult to abandon at later stages. We now explore these mental traps, how they impact our thinking, and what we can do about them.

Sunk Costs   Economists tell us the resources we have already put into a project or idea that are not recoverable are *sunk costs* and should not dictate our future course of action. Unfortunately, human experience shows that we rarely are able to distance ourselves from these investments. Once we have put in any sort of resources, we want to leverage them, not forget about them. Our investments are not only monetary. Time, ego, cognitive effort, reputation, emotion—these are all investments that can be even harder to relinquish than monetary investments. Often we continue to allocate resources to justify a previous commitment, whether or not it still makes sense to do so. Suppose you buy a nonrefundable ticket to a concert, but find yourself sick in bed on the day of the show. How many times have you dragged yourself out of bed only because you already bought the ticket, and then sat miserably in the theater, wishing you were home with some hot tea? Instead, on the day of the show, you should ask yourself, "If I was going to buy a ticket today, would I do it?" If the answer is no, then stay in bed! The only decision you have is whether to have a miserable or comfortable evening; the money is already spent either way.

How many students invest time and effort in a professional program to earn a degree that will allow them to work in their chosen field, only to discover once they are in the workplace that they made a mistake? Instead of investigating what they could do to find a more fulfilling career, they look to the past and the sunk costs of their education, and stick with their disappointing choice. Likewise, business teams weigh how much they have already dedicated to a project and cling to these ventures even after it becomes clear that it would be wisest to discontinue their efforts. CEOs of ailing companies are often replaced, and one might wonder why a person who was smart enough to be offered the job can now be traded so quickly for another. An underlying reason is that boards assume that a new CEO will not be tied to the sunk costs incurred by a predecessor and will be able to more easily shift course. In his memoirs, Andy Grove relates the angst he felt in the 1980s when Intel's command of the memory chip business declined due to competition from Japan.[14] For months he wrestled with the dilemma of what to do. The situation continued to deteriorate, and Grove was at risk of being replaced. In the midst of this turmoil, Intel cofounder Gordon Moore came to Grove's office, and Grove asked him, if the board were to replace them, what would the new guy do? Moore responded that the new guy would get out of the memory chip business. Andy Grove resolved at that moment to be the new guy.

Loss Aversion   Sunk costs are hard to ignore, in large part because we are loss averse.[15] Walking away from a sunk cost is a loss, and we prefer not to feel the pain, so once committed to a plan we may stick with it for all the wrong reasons, not because it is the best path into the future. One of the best examples of loss aversion is people failing to sell an investment when it is worth less than what they paid. We are more sensitive to losses than to gains, and feel the pain of a loss more deeply than we feel the pleasure from an equivalent gain. Imagine that Ann and Ken inherited stock portfolios yesterday, and when they wake up today each portfolio is worth $4 million dollars. However, when they went to sleep yesterday, Ann's portfolio was worth $5 million dollars and Ken's portfolio was worth $3 million dollars. Objectively they are each $4 million dollars richer from the inheritance, but would you rather be Ann or Ken?

Policy makers have found ingenious ways to leverage the human desire to avoid loss. For example, attempts to use financial incentives for teachers to improve student achievements (merit pay for student performance) have generally not been effective. However, paying teachers a bonus in advance—knowing they will have to give the money back if students don't improve—is a much more successful strategy for increasing student test scores. Teacher incentives framed as losses resulted in as much as a 10-percentile-point increase in scores compared to students with similar backgrounds whose teachers were offered the bonus as a gain at the end of the school year.[16]

Risk Aversion   Once we own something, we often act so as not to lose, and this can lead to risk aversion. When there are two possibilities requiring that we weigh gains and losses, people will often make the choice that demonstrates a preference for avoiding losses over making gains. However, in avoiding what we perceive as risk, we might fail to consider the opportunity cost of not taking an action. In a scare that reverberates to this day, a British doctor, Andrew Wakefield, published a paper in 1998 claiming he had evidence that the measles, mumps, and rubella vaccine might cause symptoms of autism. In England, thousands of parents refused to vaccinate their children, resulting in hundreds of hospitalizations and even deaths after children contracted the diseases that the vaccination was designed to prevent. Since then, at least 20 controlled studies have found no link between vaccines and autism, and an independent review concluded that Wakefield had been fraudulent and irresponsible in his research. In 2004, 10 of the 13 authors of the Wakefield study retracted it; the Lancet, the prestigious medical journal that published the article, also retracted it; and in 2010, the British government revoked Wakefield's license to practice medicine. Yet the belief among a sizeable number of parents in the United Kingdom and the United States has persisted, propagated by celebrity figures such as actress Jenny McCarthy, who believes her son's autism may have been caused by vaccines. In the minds of these parents, avoiding anything that carries any perceived risk of autism can seem safer than opting for a vaccine against diseases that seem unlikely. Yet the reality is that the incidence of these potentially life-threatening diseases is on the rise.[17] Choosing not to get a vaccine is not a risk-free choice, but parents seem to frame it as such. Not taking action in order to avoid one risk may unwittingly put us on a collision course with another, even greater risk.

A great advantage of deliberate chaos is that it helps to mitigate problems of sunk costs and loss aversion that lead to unwarranted or misplaced risk aversion. In the stage of deliberate chaos we are not invested yet, thus preventing an early attachment to an idea that may prove unworthy. Ongoing engagement with people who think differently may help us see possibilities even after resources have been invested, possibilities that are not easily visible to us precisely because of the sunk costs we have incurred. For Andy Grove, it was putting himself in the frame of mind of such a person, asking, "What would a new guy do?" To combat loss aversion and potentially dangerous choices as a result of risk aversion, engaging with others to frame options through more perspectives may help us make better-informed choices.

Deliberate Chaos Reduces Cycle Time

The first modern mechanical clocks in Europe were installed in town churches in the late 1200s; they had no hands, but simply had a bell that rang on the hour. People's sense of time was vague, but certainly better than in the days of no clocks at all. It was only in the 1600s that dials and minute hands were added, creating greater precision. In the last 500 years, our sense of time has changed dramatically; clocks drive activities down to units of seconds and even nanoseconds. With these advancements, our focus on time has become compulsive. People hammer the "close door" button in elevators because the doors don't shut fast enough; they abandon websites that don't load instantaneously (remember when dialup felt fast?!); drivers speed through yellow lights because the wait at the red feels interminable. In a new take on "fast food," the restaurant of a Marriot Hotel where we recently ate had segmented its menu not into the usual categories (appetizers, entrees, desserts), but based on time; the three parts of the menu were labeled Below 5, Under 10, and Quick 20, referring to the number of minutes it would take to be served.

Time pressures underlie every project, and milestone targets loom. Yet to engage with others before embarking on idea execution takes time. With projects operating under stringent deadlines, with the itch to feel that we are making progress, how can we afford to take the time to create deliberate chaos?

Dedicating time up front to engage others will actually end up saving time. Exploring more options before deciding on a solution gives us the opportunity to identify possibilities that perhaps are not immediately obvious, but may be much faster to execute with no compromise to quality. It ultimately takes less time to deal with errors in the early stages, alleviating a later need to undo and redo work to fix emergent problems. Leaders who have adopted this approach have found that projects are often finished ahead of schedule, beating their own deadlines.

Deliberate Chaos Creates Build-in

Projects that involve the investment of multiple stakeholders typically get to a point where buy-in is needed. The stakes may be high, and uncertainty looms because key people may not buy in. Wouldn't it be terrific if you never had to seek buy-in again?! The people whose buy-in you will need are precisely the people whose perceptions you want to get very early, in the stage of deliberate chaos. Instead of assuming what they might say down the road, involve them in the development stages, taking their input into account, and building their concerns into your plan. You are effectively reducing the uncertainty about what they will say because you don't wait to hear it. Instead of trying to get buy-in later (with great uncertainty about whether you will be successful), start by creating "build-in."[18] The results can be dramatic, turning a potential future adversary into an established ally.

As an example, in the early 1980s a group of three scientists had discovered a new drug, and they wanted to create a pharmaceutical company. Naïve and inexperienced, they contacted the FDA to ask how to get started. The person who answered their call probably fell out of his or her chair. In those days the relationship between the FDA and pharmaceutical companies was decidedly adversarial. Companies would identify a drug, conduct animal and human research (which took an average of seven years), and then box up the data and send them to the FDA for approval. The FDA might take as long as two years to review the data, and then they invariably would ask for more research. The average amount of time it took to move from drug discovery to final drug approval was about 12 years, with much of the delay due to FDA requests for more information. Pharmaceutical companies were frustrated because the patent on a drug was only good for 17 years, and the clock starts ticking from the day of discovery. Each day of delay was one less day to make money, so you can imagine how antagonistic these companies felt toward the FDA.

Now enter these three scientists, calling the FDA for advice! Developing a relationship with the FDA from the very beginning of their process, they asked if they could continue to call as the research progressed, to get the input of these inspectors rather than wait to box up their data at the end of the research to get feedback. The FDA agreed. By involving the FDA early and on an ongoing basis, never guessing what the inspector might say but instead asking questions throughout to eliminate uncertainty and the need to later redo or add more research, Epogen, for the treatment of anemia, was approved in just seven years, and created the success story that has become Amgen.[19]

Deliberate Chaos Example: The Agile Project System

Software developers have evolved a methodology to help them embrace constant change and reduce complexity. Traditional project development meant performing activities in a predetermined sequence; designing and building an entire project over many months, with stages and milestones, sign-offs and handoffs, and only testing for flaws when the final product was ready. The result was costly, slow, and error laden.

Software developers now use a system of rapid prototyping, termed "agile development," that enables them to test a product and quickly create successive improvements based on user feedback and observations of how well the product meets its purpose. Agile development means that smaller segments of the software are developed and tested in shorter cycles of days or weeks. Rapid feedback and ongoing collaboration with customers is built in. Members of agile teams communicate regularly and openly with each other about new findings as the project develops; one of the rules is a focus on people rather than process. The result is far fewer surprises at the end of the project, because more errors are found early when they are easier to eliminate, mitigate, or fix.

Visit the Future

The writer William Gibson has authored several works of science fiction, depicting all sorts of imaginary future worlds. He has also been credited with the following quote:

The future is already here. It's just not evenly distributed.[20]

This statement was a game changer in our thinking. The more we thought about it, the more we realized that Gibson was on to something extraordinary. What could this mean in a world where we are trying to conquer uncertainty? If Gibson was right, it would mean that to bring the future to the present, you could go looking for it in places it might already exist. Your ambiguous and fuzzy future might already be part of someone else's concrete and vivid present state. You could then go and visit your own future, gaining clarity and reducing uncertainty. Gibson's idea is not science fiction but is the reality of our world. Over the last few years we have helped numerous people, teams, and organizations find ways to visit their own future to conquer uncertainty.

One of Iris's daughters became enamored with archeology while in high school. A teacher had ignited her imagination with the adventure of working on digs and she envisioned a career in the field. Would it be possible for her to visit this dream? During one of her high school summers she had an opportunity to experience an excavation, and she soon came to realize that a life of digging through sand in the hot sun, day after day, was definitely not for her. Visiting the future helped her to correct what turned out to be misplaced assumptions. Unfortunately, too many people pursue a career believing it's what they want and, after training and investment, find themselves in a reality that makes them miserable.

The current trend of college students pursuing internships to explore potentially interesting career paths is an excellent way for them to visit the future and check their assumptions. Adults who are already stuck in jobs they don't like can also visit alternative futures. A company called Vocation Vacations was started in 2003 to match people who want to change careers with mentors who have those careers. During time off from their current job, people spend a few days working with or shadowing someone in another field to learn more about it. Today the company is called Pivot Planet, and has mentors in more than 200 fields, ranging from acupuncturists to wedding planners, to advise others looking to pivot from an existing career to a new one.[21] Visiting the future can sometimes help to confirm what we want; sometimes we discover that what we think we want is not what we want at all; and sometimes, what we think we don't want is actually exactly what we want. We like to think of these visits to the future as "mini-max investments": minimal investments of time and resources, leading to maximal gains in certainty.

There are inspiring examples of organizations that have visited their own futures and created extraordinary outcomes from what they learned. In the early 1990s, Mexican cement manufacturer Cemex was in turmoil. Customers had no idea when their orders might be filled. Dispatchers taking orders would agree to whatever delivery time a customer requested but, in reality, the delivery might arrive late or, more likely, not at all. Trucks breaking down, lost paperwork, traffic gridlock, bad weather, unstable labor relations, and any number of other variables could interfere with delivery; as a result, fewer than 35 percent of orders were delivered on time. To counter such uncertainty, often customers would place multiple separate orders for each delivery, hoping that one of the trucks would show up. Cemex was on the verge of bankruptcy. Desperate to improve their on-time delivery, Cemex visited the future.

Cemex executives asked themselves who on this planet was already excellent at on-time delivery, and their first visit was to FedEx. Why FedEx? Cemex was not looking to benchmark themselves against others in the concrete business; they were looking for lessons from experts on the attribute they needed to improve. Dazzled by the lessons they learned from FedEx, they then visited Domino's Pizza. At the time, Domino's had a promise to deliver every order within 30 minutes or the pizza would be free, and Cemex needed insights on how they made that happen in a world of uncertainty. Here, they learned yet more lessons on their path to improve their own delivery process. Their final visit, to a 911 dispatch center in Houston, revealed the underlying principle that would enable them to eliminate and reduce uncertainty where possible and embrace uncertainty as needed. The 911 principle states that although each individual emergency is unpredictable, emergencies as a category occur in sufficient number to discern patterns, and patterns can be predicted and planned for. Cemex resolved to understand the patterns of its marketplace, and to respond in real time to the changing needs of customers as individual demands arose. Within a few months, Cemex was delivering 98 percent of its orders on time. They created a delivery model aligned with the framework of *adaptive planning*; we will continue the Cemex story when we explain the adaptive planning method of embracing uncertainty later in this chapter.[22]

Beyond visiting the future, it is also possible to partner with and for the future.

Partnering

One of the ways to conquer uncertainty, and make your own weakness irrelevant, is to partner. Partnering takes many forms including developing relationships with other stakeholders, collaborating with people who are closer to the future than you, as well as making deals with your future self.

Good-bye, Public Relations; Hello, Relationships with the Public

In complex systems, stakeholders impact outcomes. A stakeholder is any group or person who either touches the system or will be touched by the system, even indirectly. Even those who we think are only touched by the system can surprise us by turning around to touch the system, influencing its behavior.

One such group or stakeholder is "the public." The field of public relations is predicated on the notion that the mind of the public can be sculpted and shaped if we just use the right tools. Persuasion research and choice-architecture frameworks teach us how to present information to others in order to influence them and get them to agree with our way of thinking. The problem is that in a Google world, everyone has access to information about these tactics. The public is increasingly connected to others in their network who can call out unfair or manipulative tactics. Relying on public relations to get compliance and buy-in has become increasingly ineffective as a strategy for solving complex issues. Far more valuable is to develop trusted relationships with the public, building stakeholders into the problem-solving process.

When NASA officials wanted to close a nuclear reactor facility in Ohio, they realized that many local residents were unaware that there even was a nuclear reactor on the site, and that learning about it would be an unpleasant surprise. They knew the neighbors would have deep concerns about safety, but that ongoing community support would be critical in the effort to decommission the site. A Community Involvement Plan was charted and a group of respected community members were tapped to be the trusted source of information for other residents. This committee of local residents included teachers, religious leaders, environmental activists, health professionals, and neighbors living close to the facility, who met regularly with NASA officials to raise questions and help solve problems. For example, NASA made it known that they wanted to move waste through the south side of the site, thinking neighbors would appreciate that the trucks would not be going through residential areas. However, the community partners voiced concern that the trucks would be passing a school, and requested another route. NASA complied by building a gate on the east side of the property, which diverted traffic away from both residential areas and the school. By involving the community early, NASA was more easily able to accommodate their requests, and the public felt that they had a voice in the process, making them more comfortable with the project as it evolved. In addition, all local residents were invited to tour the NASA facility, become familiar with the site, and learn about the safety precautions NASA was prioritizing for the project. NASA established a Community Information Bank at the local library, with copies of all project plans, reports, and documents updated throughout the project and available freely to whomever was interested. (A project website was also set up, but this was the year 2000, so many people were not yet Internet connected!)

The effort to partner with the public created a trusted relationship between NASA and the local residents. By building a "trust bank," NASA was able to avert disaster when low levels of contamination were unexpectedly found in a residential area quite a distance away, apparently due to a ditch and a brook flowing near the fence of the NASA site. Officials immediately made the community aware of the problem and what they were planning to do. Because residents were already trusted partners in the project, they allowed NASA to take the needed steps without interference. As NASA officials put it, they were able to take a withdrawal from the trust bank, because they had made enough deposits into the account from the start of the project. NASA officials had realized that they would be far more successful if they partnered with the community, and in so doing, they turned a potential future adversary into an ally.[23]

Make Weakness Irrelevant

Other organizations have also partnered to reduce the uncertainty of the future, and to make their own weaknesses irrelevant. For example, even though Netflix has a lot of smart software specialists working for them, around the world there are even more smart software specialists that don't work for them. When Netflix wanted to develop an algorithm to better predict which movies customers might want to see based on what they had already ordered, they turned it into a global competition, offering one million dollars to the winning team. Thousands tackled the problem for more than three years until finally two of the outside teams partnered with each other and earned the prize.[24]

For a more structured partnering arrangement, InnoCentive is a forum for matching problem owners with problem solvers. Organizations can post their most difficult challenges and connect with millions of problem solvers from multiple disciplines. Solvers who submit winning solutions earn monetary rewards and the problem owners attain the rights to the intellectual property. The Cleveland Clinic, The Rockefeller Foundation, and NASA are just three of the hundreds of organizations that have partnered with external talent through InnoCentive. To date, more than 1,000 posted challenges have been solved. Often the most innovative solutions come from problem solvers outside the discipline connected with the challenge.[25]

Procter & Gamble innovates through InnoCentive, as well as through Connect + Develop, a program developed in-house for external partnerships. For Procter & Gamble, partnerships have been a way of life from the beginning of the company. William Procter was a candle maker; James Gamble was a soap maker. Competing for the same raw materials, they realized that they could negotiate better deals from suppliers by partnering with each other. Thus was born The Procter & Gamble Company (P&G). Throughout their history, P&G continued to partner with others to develop some of their biggest product successes: Ivory Soap, Crisco, Tide, Crest toothpaste, and Bounce fabric softener. In 2000, they felt that they wanted to do even more to foster external partnerships. The world was moving too quickly for them to keep up with technological and competitive changes. To create sustainable value, they decided to formalize a system for enhanced partnering, and called the program Connect + Develop. The goal was to generate at least half of all new products from partnerships with external collaborators. Connect + Develop has been hugely successful, helping to bring new products to market faster and at lower cost, with benefits to both P&G and its partners, as well as to consumers. P&G aspires now to be the worldwide open-innovation partner of choice.

In Chapter 2, "Connect to a Compelling Purpose," we told the story of the small Canadian lumber town of Chemainus that reframed its purpose. It is also a story of a successful partnership. To keep the town alive following the decline of its key employer, Chemainus residents rallied together and invented a new vision for the future by partnering with artists who transformed the town into an outdoor art gallery. With over 40 murals covering exterior walls of public buildings, it has become a destination for thousands of curious tourists, and has turned Chemainus into a thriving economic community. Through its partnerships with artists, Chemainus reinvented its identity from dying lumber town to flourishing arts district.

Find Partners Who Are One Step Closer to the Future Than You

The "six degrees of separation" concept posits that any two people on the planet are six or fewer social links apart from one another. You are one degree away from all the people you know, two degrees away from everyone that they know, and so on. In 1994, students in Pennsylvania invented the game Six Degrees of Kevin Bacon, creating a movie trivia challenge to connect every known film actor to Bacon in six cast lists or fewer, where in two actors are connected if they have appeared in a movie together. The game popularized the six-degree concept and, since then, attempts have been made to verify the validity of the idea. Microsoft analyzed billions of electronic messages sent through their instant messaging network in June 2006, which was about half the instant messaging traffic in the world at that time, and announced that the average separation between any two people was a fraction over six links. Columbia University experimented with the idea in 2003 and also estimated that the average length was right around six.[26] The phrase "six degrees" has come to represent the idea of a small world, intricately connected and bound, irrespective of geography and other boundaries.

We can leverage the web of connectedness to partner with others who are more closely linked to those whose help we need. Barack Obama's 2008 campaign team knew they needed to win Florida and leveraged young voters with whom they had a direct link, asking them to mediate a connection with their grandparents. The "Great Schlep" became the organizing engine to mobilize the visits of young supporters into the living rooms of their grandparents in Florida to talk them out of voting for John McCain. The state went to Obama.[27]

This strategy was a huge shift from the typical experience we go through before elections. For most of us, the weeks before an election bring an incessant barrage of phone calls from campaign volunteers, urging us to vote for whomever the unknown caller is supporting. If you are like us, you hang up as quickly as you can, and eagerly wait for Election Day so that the nuisance calls will stop. It's really quite a wasted effort, since calls from strangers rarely influence people anyway. As the Obama campaign demonstrated, hearing the message from family and friends is far more effective.

In 2012, the Obama campaign team built on their 2008 strategy and leveraged Facebook to reach more weakly affiliated voters. Instead of volunteers calling random people, they created the digital version of a trusted friend knocking on your door and asking you to support their candidate. Obama supporters who signed up for the Facebook app gave the campaign permission to look at their Facebook friends list. The campaign called this strategy "targeted sharing," and asked supporters to send targeted messages to specific friends. More than 600,000 supporters responded, clicking their requests to more than 5 million contacts, asking their friends to vote, register to vote, or watch a video designed to change their mind. The strategy was a game changer, resulting in significant impact on voter behavior.[28]

Businesses can also leverage the concept of degrees of separation to get closer to noncustomers. The car company Acura analyzed the profile of their typical customer and found that many of them stay at W Hotels when traveling. It occurred to them that there might be many people who stay at W Hotels who don't know about Acura or don't think of it when considering a car purchase. Partnering with W Hotels, Acura now offers a complimentary car service to guests who need transportation within a 5-mile radius of the hotel. In fact, if a guest shows enough interest in the car, the driver may loan them the car to drive during their stay, asking only that they leave the keys with the concierge when they check out. Acura is transforming a two-degree-of-separation connection with potential future customers (Acura is linked to W Hotels, and W Hotels is linked to these guests) into a more direct, one-degree-of-separation relationship by partnering with W Hotels. Acura reports that the program has been a resounding success in turning chauffeured guests into car owners.[29]

Partner with Your Future Self

As mentioned earlier, we as individuals can partner with others to reduce uncertainty and increase our potential for success. For example, working with a mentor is often recommended as a strategy for personal growth. In choosing your mentors, look for people who already embody the attributes you want to develop. In effect, working with a mentor is a way of partnering with your future self.

Sometimes, you don't need another person to form a partnership. Your present self can partner with your future self. For example, Sophie has a terrible weakness for birthday cakes (the corner piece with all the extra frosting, please!). She knows herself well enough to know that by the time evening arrives, she will eat any leftover birthday cake in the house, whether it's good for her or not. She has plenty of willpower in the morning, but none in the evening. So, her best morning self partners with her weak evening self, and if there is a cake in the house, "morning Sophie" gets rid of the cake before breakfast, knowing that "evening Sophie" will be unable to do so.[30]

Indulging in too much birthday cake may be an idiosyncratic weakness, but a more common and serious weakness affecting many people is failing to save enough money in the present for future retirement. Even though many people want to save more, they just don't do it. One of the reasons we use our money today instead of saving some of it for the future is that our future selves feel like strangers to us because of the uncertainty of who we will be and what we will want and need. In fact, neuroscientists have found that when we think about our future selves, the same brain regions are activated as when we think about strangers.[31] It's hard to sacrifice money today for the unclear needs of the future, especially if we feel disconnected from this future self. We would rather spend on the current "us" than save money to give it to a future "stranger!" A surprising number of people even fail to participate in retirement plans set up by their employer, often foregoing matching funds.

To make it easier to partner with the future self that needs money for retirement, economists are developing interventions that help the present self make better choices in partnership with the future self. One such tool is Save More Tomorrow (SMarT), a savings plan devised by Richard Thaler of the University of Chicago and Shlomo Benartzi of UCLA that has had great success.[32] Employees commit to join a company retirement-savings plan, but their actual contributions only start with their next pay raise. They enroll in the program in the present but it does not cost them any of their current salary, so they don't feel they are giving up money that they need right now. Once they get a pay raise, a certain percentage is automatically allocated to the retirement account, and the contribution rate continues to rise automatically with each successive pay raise.

This strategy actually leverages the fact that it is hard for us to imagine the future. A future pay raise is less tangible and harder to imagine than money we have now, so it is easier to be generous and allocate a portion of it to our future self. In the first rollout of the program, almost 80 percent of people offered the plan joined. Of those who joined, 80 percent remained in the program through their fourth pay raise (the length of the study), and average saving rates increased from 3.5 percent to 13.6 percent over 40 months. The program is now offered by more than half of the large retirement plans in the United States, and is incorporated in the Pension Protection Act of 2006.[33]

Another tool now available is a virtual time machine that morphs pictures of people into an age-progressed image, or even an avatar, of their future self. A person who is in their twenties can interact with a vivid, realistic rendering of themselves at 70. Initial experiments show that people who interact with their virtual older selves allocate significantly more money to savings for the future.[34]

Embrace Uncertainty

Bringing the future to the present may enable us to eliminate and reduce some aspects of uncertainty. However, there is no method to eradicate all uncertainty. Instead of ignoring or fighting uncertainty, we need a system to embrace it and thrive. To embrace uncertainty means that instead of trying to create plans for every contingency, we create a plan that includes a readiness to adapt as the future unfolds.

Zara, the clothing chain from Spain, upended the fashion industry by creating an adaptive business model in an otherwise competitive landscape of rigid planning. While other brands update their offerings once a season, Zara brings the future to the present with updated new designs twice a week. They study customer demand with real-time sales data, and store managers help shape designs with daily reports about what customers are asking for. It takes the company only weeks to come up with a new item from design to delivery, a process that takes months for their competitors. This gives the company more flexibility to respond to notoriously fickle fashion trends and, in so doing, reduces the uncertainty of customer demand for their product. When Madonna performed a concert series in Spain, fans were able to come to her last performance wearing the outfit Madonna had worn at the first concert.[35] What is the secret to becoming as nimble as Zara? Let's start with a lesson from the U.S. military.

Commander's Intent

One of the most oft-repeated axioms of war is that no battle plan ever survives contact with the enemy. There is no way to know in advance everything that will happen once the battle starts, so the uncertainties of war demand that plans be flexible and adapt to the facts as they unfold on the ground. Fully aware that it is not possible to plan for every contingency, military leaders include Commander's Intent when describing battle plans to the forces that will carry out the mission. Commander's Intent is a statement of purpose and a way to lead amid uncertainty. It succinctly describes what the end state should look like and the parameters of success. With everyone clear on Commander's Intent, individual initiative becomes possible as the battle moves forward and plans become irrelevant or obsolete; troops are able to exploit changes in circumstances instead of being paralyzed by them. Military plans without a clearly stated Commander's Intent can quickly spiral into chaos when forces are not clear about what the plan is supposed to accomplish. Any unexpected obstacle that throws the plan off course becomes the trigger for disaster, because troops have no framework for assessing how to react.

The same foundations for leading in uncertainty can be deployed within nonmilitary organizations. Executive Intent in the corporate world needs to be as clear as Commander's Intent in the military: a statement of purpose that draws us into the future, with a clearly defined set of standards that guide decisions and behavior. Organizations with a clear and compelling statement of purpose combined with strong standards are able to remain agile, cope with uncertainty, and adapt to the future as it unfolds far more effectively than those that only focus on rigid tactics, processes, and procedures.

Adaptive Planning

A useful metaphor to distinguish between rigid planning that ignores uncertainty and adaptive planning that embraces uncertainty comes from the world of transportation. The U.S. railroad system, engineered in the late 1800s, is an example of a rigid planning model. Thousands of miles of tracks were laid to connect towns and cities across the country. However, to enable trains coming from opposite directions to use a single track, the innovative idea of a sidetrack was devised. Trains heading toward each other would meet just in time to pass using the side track. For the system to succeed, however, train drivers had to adhere to their schedules to avoid delays and possible collisions.

The system was so rigid that time itself had to be recalibrated for the railroad companies.[36] Before the era of the trains; there were hundreds of time zones in the United States! Every town calibrated "high noon" based on the time that the sun was directly overhead. It might be noon in Philadelphia, but it was possibly 12:17 in New York City and 12:33 in Boston. This made scheduling so difficult that in 1883 the rail companies created Standard Railway Time and divided the country into the four continental time zones we know today. Tailored to the demands of the train schedules, the strangely zigzagged division of the country was designed to benefit railroad timetables. The federal government soon officially standardized time based on the railroad division of the country (to this day, all time-related issues are handled by the Department of Transportation). The railroad system was so inflexible that anything that came into contact with it had to adapt because the system itself could not.

In contrast to railroads, the model used by taxicabs is highly adaptive. With trains, passengers have to go to fixed stations, trains depart at fixed times, and they move along fixed routes. Taxis have none of this rigidity and are able to adapt to the needs of customers. A taxi can pick you up wherever you happen to be, at any hour, and take the best route available at the time to get you to your destination. Should you change your mind mid-route and want to go somewhere else, the driver can adapt to this as well. The taxicab model embraces uncertainty and responds as the future unfolds to best meet customer needs. The railroad model says, "This is who we are and we can't do it any other way—take it or leave it." The taxicab model asks, "What can we do for you to create value?"

From Railroad to Taxicab

Let's return to Cemex, the Mexican cement company that visited its future to save itself from bankruptcy. Cemex was an old company, founded in 1906, and it had worked itself into railroad-type thinking. Customers were required to place their orders at least two days before delivery. That meant that customers had to guess when they actually would need the perishable product, and on the day of delivery many customers would cancel or reschedule their orders. Cemex had tried to force its customers to stick with their orders by imposing financial penalties for changes, but to no avail. They tried imposing longer lead times, requiring customers to call them one week before delivery instead of two days, but if anything, that only exacerbated their problems. Instead of bringing the future closer to the present to reduce uncertainty, asking for longer lead times distanced Cemex from the future delivery date and increased uncertainty.

Cemex executives began to question their entire model. How could they organize to bring the future closer to the present, and embrace the uncertainty of their chaotic marketplace rather than continue fighting it? Instead of punishing customers with penalties or forcing them to abide by the schedule Cemex had preordained, Cemex decided to embrace last-minute changes as part of the plan. As noted earlier, they visited FedEx, a model of on-time delivery; Domino's, which could deliver a perishable product on time; and finally, Houston's 911 dispatch center, which at the time had an average response time of 4 minutes. From these visits Cemex learned about the flexibility of adaptive planning, a model of thinking that enables response to an environment that changes so quickly, no rigid, advanced planning could possibly anticipate and respond to it.

Instead of keeping all the ready-mix cement trucks in fixed locations inside the manufacturing plants, Cemex adopted the taxicab model, distributing trucks to roam the city. Just as taxicabs don't roam at random (they are more likely to circulate near airports, convention centers, and hotels), Cemex could track where building permits had been pulled and new construction started, so they knew where likely customers were centered and positioned trucks accordingly. Drivers were given authority to make on-the-spot, just-in-time decisions about their ability to deliver on time. For example, if an order came in to headquarters and GPS data showed that Truck 27 was closest to the site, that driver could update and augment GPS data by informing headquarters that an accident had just occurred, he was now stuck, and that Truck 39, while appearing farther away, would be able to deliver faster.

Cemex committed to a delivery model of same-day service and free, unlimited order changes. In fact, if product failed to arrive within

20 minutes of the promised delivery time, the customer would get a discount. On-time delivery quickly reached 98 percent and, in the years since, Cemex has become one of the largest cement and concrete companies in the world, operating in over 60 countries across North America, the Caribbean, South America, Europe, Asia, and Africa. In every new marketplace they bring their adaptive thinking to satisfy customer needs. They simplify wherever possible, to reduce uncertainty across marketplaces. For example, around the world, in every Cemex plant, pipes carrying natural gas are painted one color, and pipes carrying air are painted another color. This makes it easier for transferred or visiting employees to quickly integrate into the plant, and reduces errors. Standardizations are never etched in stone; employees are encouraged to suggest improvements, new ideas are tested, and when effective, results are disseminated worldwide.

CEO Lorenzo Zambrano has empowered his workforce with transparent access to information, and insists that they adhere to three core standards that are the Cemex Way: *collaboration* (with customers, colleagues, suppliers, and other partners), *integrity* (acting with honesty, responsibility, and respect at all times), and *leadership* (envisioning the future and focusing efforts on service excellence, sustainability, and innovation). Their planning model can successfully be adapted to new environments because they adhere to an unwavering set of core principles and standards. These are not rigid rules, but rather strict principles through which workers can adapt to the changing needs of the customer as the future unfolds. The values and standards are universal, and Cemex employees are empowered to act on them while respecting the local consumer and local marketplace. The standards are the anchors of stability amidst incessant change, and provide the basis for partnerships and initiatives, new products, and novel services. In this way, Cemex has taken a commodity like concrete and developed remarkable customer-focused innovations like bacteria-resistant concrete for hospitals and salt-resistant concrete for harbors.

Cemex has grown into a global powerhouse in part through strategic acquisitions in Latin America, Europe, and the United States, but its real power has come from how well those acquired companies have been integrated into the Cemex Way and have become part of the culture that Zambrano calls "One Cemex." Zambrano believes that clear core values and articulated ethical standards are critical for success, especially as Cemex has expanded into other countries, not all of which embrace those values or uphold them as social norms.

To reinforce its values and the adaptive mind-set, Cemex's weekly meetings start with the question, "What did we learn last week that will help us be better next week?" The question fosters a focus on relentless improvement for customer satisfaction. In addition, conversations about ethics and ethical dilemmas are part of monthly executive meetings between Cemex headquarters and country managers, to ensure that upholding company values overrides any other consideration, even if it means losing business. In one instance, a top sales performer caught pilfering unused products was fired, even though it meant the organization would probably have trouble meeting its sales objectives for that year.[37]

In 2003, *Wired* magazine ranked Cemex one of the world's top five "masters of innovation, technology, and strategic vision" for their just-in-time delivery system. In 2008, they placed Cemex just behind Google, and ahead of eBay, in a survey of companies reshaping the global economy.[38] As of this writing, Cemex has had its share of struggles following the massive economic turmoil that started in 2008 but this, too, is likely to be more readily conquered with the adaptive mind-set and strong standards that Cemex has embraced.

Distributed Leadership

From our experience, most organizations and teams admit that they are too "railroad," and need to become more "taxicab," to better adapt to unfolding futures. In the railroad mentality, people are given responsibilities to carry out and we make them accountable to deliver on those responsibilities. To create a taxicab mentality, we have to give people one more thing: the authority to make decisions, to make sure that their job can get done even when unexpected and unforeseen contingencies arise. Every person in the organization, at their level of work, must be thought of and treated as a leader; we have to dignify the detail doers. Extraordinary success cannot be micromanaged.

A few years ago a friend told us of a ridiculous situation he encountered while driving cross-country. He and his wife were on the outskirts of Atlanta, trying to get to the city before it got late, so they didn't want to stop for dinner in a restaurant. Instead, they spotted a takeout pizza place and decided to get a pizza and eat while driving. His wife waited in the car while he walked up to the counter to order. The first thing the young woman behind the counter said to him was, "Phone number, please." This was before cell phones, so he gave his Los Angeles area phone number. She entered it into her computer, but a message popped up that it was not valid. She informed him that he needed a local number. He tried to make up a number, but the system recognized it as a fake. He then tried logic, asking why he needed to provide a phone number since he wasn't asking for delivery, but she insisted that it was the only way to sell him a pizza. The computer could not take an order without a phone number. Finally, he asked if she would be so kind as to put her own phone number into the order. At this point the young woman froze, telling him, "We have a rule that employees are not allowed to share personal information with customers." When he explained that he would not need to see the number, because it would go directly into the order, she had no idea if that would be breaking the rule or not. This young woman had been trained with a list of rules but had no authority to adapt to a situation that did not fit the predetermined process. Our friend walked out of there without a pizza.

Think about your organization, your team, your life. Are you more railroad or taxicab? Where do you need to be more railroad? Where do you need to be more taxicab? Remember, in a world of complexity you cannot micromanage, or adhere to an excessively rigid plan, and expect to shape extraordinary outcomes.

The Adaptive Plan in Action

What follows are the key elements of an adaptive strategy.

Purpose   First and foremost, what are you trying to achieve? Purpose is the difference you are trying to make. Every action and possible plan has to be evaluated against a meaningful purpose. Raising children is complexity in action, and too often parents and children get into battles of will over ultimately meaningless issues. When Iris's first child was 2 years old she was a very picky eater, and she refused to eat meat or eggs. As a new parent, Iris was elated when her daughter stood trans-fixed at a restaurant omelet station. After her daughter happily ate the cheese and olive omelet she herself had designed, Iris decided to try the same tactic at home. The next morning she offered her daughter an omelet and asked her what to include. Without any hesitation, her daughter asked for an omelet with chocolate chips. Iris's first reaction was, "Are you kidding?!" but she quickly stopped herself. Given that her underlying purpose was to get her daughter to eat eggs, would it really matter if a few chocolate chips came along for the ride? It was actually pretty good!

Herb Kelleher cofounded Southwest Airlines in 1967, when air travel was reserved for the rich. His purpose was to democratize the skies and make air travel affordable. Every decision he made was based on his purpose, which was to change the marketplace and give ordinary people the option to fly. When critics complained that Southwest had no meals, no first class, and no assigned seating, Kelleher reflected that all those things would raise costs and violate the purpose of the airline. Measured against his clear purpose, decisions were easy. More recently, many airlines started charging for bags. Consultants advised Southwest that they could make millions of dollars if they did the same. The senior leadership refused, because it violated the purpose of the company. They argued that charging for bags would make flying less accessible to people. Refusing to stray from their purpose ultimately made them more money; when they started an ad campaign with the slogan "Bags Fly Free," Southwest achieved $1 billion in new revenue and captured market share from their competitors.[39]

For an adaptive plan, purpose must be clearly articulated. Tactics are judged relative to the purpose, and as the environment changes, new tactics may be added and old ones abandoned to better support the purpose.

Assumptions   What are the underlying assumptions that are driving the plan? Different groups working on the same project may be operating from entirely different perceptions about what is important or what is true. In the context of purpose, discuss what success and failure would look like. One of the risks in our thinking is that we tend only to look for or see information that confirms our biases and assumptions; we interpret information to align with our assumptions, and ignore or forget anything that does not fit.[40] The psychologist

Abraham Maslow quipped that "if the only tool you have is a hammer, you tend to treat everything like a nail."

Confirmation bias is a well-documented flaw in thinking, and the best method of conquering it is to actively seek disconfirming evidence. None of us are immune to the trap of either ignoring or dismissing disconfirming evidence. Doctors, for example, are estimated to diagnose a patient's illness within 17 to 22 seconds of entering the examining room, and they spend the rest of the visit asking questions that confirm the diagnosis.[41] They focus on symptoms consistent with the diagnosis and ignore or downplay other symptoms. In medicine more broadly, experts believed for years that stomach ulcers were caused by stress. When evidence emerged that a bacterium was actually to blame, the initial reaction was dismissive; it took years for the medical community to accept what we now know to be the actual cause of stomach ulcers.

Confirmation bias leads to a tendency to test ideas in a one-sided way, focusing on one possibility and ignoring alternatives. To evaluate an idea, establish a viable control for comparison. NASA fell victim to confirmation bias before launching the space shuttle *Challenger* in 1986. Engineers were concerned that the O-rings, a critical component of the vehicle, were subject to damage in cold-weather launches. Out of the 30 prior shuttle launches, O-ring damage had occurred in 7, so NASA asked the engineers to submit the launch temperatures for those problem flights. The evidence was not convincing; some of the problem flights had occurred in cold weather, but others were in warm weather, so the launch was approved. *Challenger* exploded seconds after liftoff. Instead of looking at launch temperatures for the 7 problem flights, NASA should have looked at the data for all the cold weather launches and compared this information to the data from all the warm weather launches. They would have discovered that O-ring problems had occurred on every single cold weather launch. They would have also seen that the 23 successful flights with no O-ring problems were launched only in warm weather. Even in our everyday decisions about where to look for information, most of us fall victim to confirmation bias, preferring sources that affirm our beliefs. Liberals seek news from sources like MSNBC while conservatives tune in to FOX News.

One of the easiest and best ways to conquer confirmation bias is to ensure that teams are open to dissenting opinion and that those opinions are adequately explored. Unanimity or absence of dissent should raise alarm. When asking your team for a recommendation, also request information about the pros and cons of the credible alternatives they considered that were rejected. Encourage a sincere admission of uncertainty that is accounted for in the recommendations.[42]

When comparing alternatives, don't fall into the trap of OR thinking, as we discussed in Chapter 4, "Amplify the Positive." Often we assume we have to choose one option and forego others. Instead, expand with AND thinking, exploring ways to leverage the best of all possibilities. Recall the story in that chapter of the debate during the writing of the Constitution. The Founding Fathers of the United States created a bicameral government that balances equality and inequality of state representation, inventing a form of government that would be the first of its kind. If they managed to integrate two seemingly mutually exclusive alternatives (we can either be equal or unequal; how can we be both at the same time?!), then many other combinations that appear to be impossible are worth pondering.

Redundancy and Slack by Design   To embrace uncertainty, add redundancy at the points of the plan that are critical to success, and build slack into the plan to create room to accommodate surprises. Cemex has multiple trucks cruising a city in Mexico; if one is disabled, another is not far away. When we travel to lecture, we have our presentation slides on our own laptops, but we also e-mail the presentation to our host and bring them on a USB drive. Should any one system fail, the slides are still accessible. Suppose a caterer is serving burritos at a New Year's party. For a burrito, the fillings can vary but the tortilla is critical. You can build a burrito with different fillings, but you can't build a burrito without a tortilla. Running out of a filling ingredient would be unfortunate, but running out of tortillas would be a fiasco. It would behoove the caterer to focus on the crucial element and bring more tortillas than they anticipate will be needed.

As you think about your own operations and projects, ask yourself, "What are the tortillas in this plan?" Create buffers of time, budget, and resources to accommodate surprises.

Purposeful Procrastination   Think carefully about what can't wait and what *should* wait. One way to embrace uncertainty is to keep more options open longer. In a changing environment, what you think is the best option now may not be best by the time a final decision or action is required. When you make restaurant dinner reservations a week ahead, you don't place your food order at the same time. You wait until you are sitting in the restaurant, menu in hand, to make your final decision. All the more important to bring this kind of thinking into decisions that have long-term impact. A friend was recently relocated to another country and, convinced that the move was permanent, immediately bought an apartment. The move turned out to be less than what he expected, and he was now stuck with home ownership he did not want. It would have been better to temporarily rent a place, even if the rent was high, and view it as the cost of reducing uncertainty.

Multiple Options　In designing a product or solution, the typical planning process starts with a preliminary design that is then developed to create a final design. Once a preliminary design has been approved, the final design is rarely significantly different from the rough draft. There are many causes for this phenomenon. Often, we get attached to our initial thinking and want to avoid the pain of lost investment of time, effort, and ego. Remember how difficult it was for Andy Grove to extricate himself from his sunk costs and see his way out of the memory chip business? Another reason we overly commit to our initial thinking is the bias that diverts our attention from disconfirming evidence that might indicate we are wrong. We just saw in the Assumptions section how the confirmation bias kept the medical community treating ulcers as resulting from stress, and NASA engineers who had designed *Challenger*, from seeing possibilities once they had established their story. Last, the rough draft channels our thinking, making it difficult to even conceive of any other option.

A more adaptive way to handle uncertainty is to initiate a project or search for solutions by calling for multiple preliminary designs. These options can be validated, perhaps by sampling the ideas among contained test groups and getting feedback on what works and what does not. Based on lessons learned, these preliminary options may then be combined in new ways to create a final design.

To keep options open and allow changes to be made more easily as new developments arise, modular designs are excellent for adaptive planning. A modular design divides unique functions into discrete systems consisting of isolated, self-contained elements that can readily be swapped out if needed. A good example of modular design is a car. When you get a flat tire, you don't have to replace the whole car. At the same time, the design allows you to upgrade or customize your tires without affecting the rest of the car. Car designers can also upgrade models from year to year without starting from scratch. Modular design combines the advantages of standardization with the flexibility of customization.

Hospitals have started to adopt the modular design concept as facilities rapidly become outdated and unable to adapt to new technologies. Instead of trying to predict where healthcare is headed, designers want to create hospitals that can adapt to whatever happens. Flexible designs allow them to move forward with construction without the fear of taking a wrong step that might obstruct future strategic initiatives. For example, at Parkland Memorial Hospital in Dallas, building designers have factored the uncertainty of the future into the blueprints. Three types of patient bed zones—for trauma, surgical, and women/infant specialty health—are interconnected so that growth in one service area can expand into an adjacent area as demand changes and patient demographics ebb and flow. With an eye toward purposeful procrastination, several empty spaces will be kept ready throughout the hospital to accommodate future technologies and new medical procedures (essentially building slack into the design), as current medical procedures become obsolete.[43]

Businesses that operate in highly uncertain environments typically test concurrent options simultaneously. Venture capital firms (which have success rates under 20 percent) and pharmaceutical companies (which run hundreds of experiments on different molecular combinations before coming up with a viable drug) are two examples. Keeping multiple options open can start with the simplest of things. How many times have you argued with your kids just as you are leaving the house that they need to put on a sweater because it might get cold? Better to just say, "Throw a sweater in your bag to keep your options open."

Positive Deviance In Chapter 4 we described the use of positive deviance to eradicate childhood malnutrition in rural Vietnam, focusing on the habits of healthy families to transform the lives of starving children, and on its application at the Pittsburgh VA Hospital to reduce hospital-acquired infections. More broadly, seeking positive deviance is a search for outliers who have found a way to create value. In predictable, complicated systems we optimize averages, and outliers indicate error or random variance. In complex systems that include a great deal of unpredictability, outliers matter because they may represent new truths we need to know about.

Within any complex system, the outliers of positive deviance can help the entire system evolve and adapt. These outliers may be people who have already detected emerging trends, teams standing on the edge of the future with a perspective that people closer to the core do not yet see, or ideas for value creation that are already being successfully implemented at a local level. Seek out and identify positive deviance and augment it by broadcasting it to all constituents, creating incentives for others to adopt a change in thinking or behavior. Positive deviants may be hiding in plain sight, and by throwing light on them the total system adapts more quickly and effectively.

The positive deviance approach has been applied in public health, nutrition, law enforcement, education, and businesses around the world.[44] A Danish prison applied the concept to enhance the resilience of prison guards.[45] Working in a highly stressful environment often causes high levels of absenteeism and turnover, and the Danish prison was trying to solve this problem amongst their guards. Previous efforts, like stricter penalties for missed work days or incentives to seek mental health services, had no effect. Officials in the system formed a positive deviance research team to observe the behavior of guards with fewer than five days of missed work, to see if there was something they were missing. It turned out to be a very simple behavioral difference. When inmates first arrive at the prison, protocol calls for the guards to gather background information, and the most common method was an interrogation type of interview. The positive deviants, however, used another method. These guards offered inmates a tour of the prison facility and, along the way, engaged them in conversation to gather the information. This small difference had a huge impact on both guards and prisoners. Inmates under the supervision of these guards were better behaved and more likely to enroll in treatment programs, and the guards were better able to handle the stress of working in the prison.

Positive deviance helps to redraw the relationships between parts of a complex system and encourages distributed leadership. The question to ask is, "Who are the positive deviants in my organization and how can they help lead us into the future?"

Make It Simple

What do Albert Einstein, Leonardo da Vinci, Henry David Thoreau, Frédéric Chopin, and Leo Tolstoy all have in common? They all had something to say about simplicity.

Everything should be as simple as possible, but no simpler.

—Einstein

Simplicity is the ultimate sophistication.

—daVinci

Our life is frittered away by detail. . . . Simplify, simplify, simplify!

—Thoreau

Simplicity is the final achievement.

—Chopin

There is no greatness where there is no simplicity.

—Tolstoy

Paradox of Choice   Complexity confuses us and paralyzes action. Been to the supermarket lately? Whatever product you need, there are dozens of choices and an array of options to choose from. Even lowly toothpaste is now offered in mind-numbing combinations of textures (paste? gel? paste plus gel?), flavors (mint? cinnamon? orange? anise?), and attributes (whitening? pro-enamel? anticavity? sensitive teeth?). The ever-increasing pool of choices in all aspects of our lives has created a dizzying number of options we have to filter through daily. On the surface, it would seem that with more choices, we can make more satisfying decisions. Yet evidence suggests otherwise. In a classic experiment, researchers went into a supermarket and displayed samples of jams for customers to taste. In one condition of the study, they displayed 6 different jams; in the other condition, 24 jams were laid out. When presented with 6 types of jam, 30 percent chose to purchase one of them, in contrast to only 3 percent of shoppers who purchased a jam from the table of 24. This type of study has been repeated with other types of products and services, including 401(k) investments, Medicare prescription drug options, and even speed dating, with similar results.[46] Faced with too many options, we often give up and choose nothing at all.

Decision experts agree that too many choices can be overwhelming when it leads to information overload. It's too simplistic to conclude that more choice is bad, but it will depend on what information we are given, the format in which the information is presented, our expertise in the domain, and how important we deem the decision to be. When information is confusing and options appear to be too similar, when we have limited expertise in the domain, or we deem the decision too important to just guess, we often become unable to make a choice. With limited cognitive resources that quickly become depleted as we try to process our options, decision fatigue may lead to choices that are not in our long-term best interest.

Understanding factors that constrain decision making can help architects of choice structure and facilitate the decision-making process. Creating defaults of opting in, rather than opting out, doesn't take away choices, but can guide us, or nudge us, into wiser ones. In an investigation into new hires choosing to join an organization's 401(k) retirement plan, the way the choice was offered made a huge difference in the decision of the employee. If employees had to enroll in the program (the default was nonenrollment), then only around 20 percent of new hires opted in within the first three months on the job, and that number only grew to about 65 percent when they were checked a few years later. However, if the default was automatic enrollment (with the clear option that the employee can opt out should they choose to do so), very few opted out; after several years, an average of 98 percent were still enrolled.[47]

We can nudge ourselves into better choices as well. For example, to clear our homes of clutter, experts recommend removing everything from your home and then deciding item by item what to bring back in. The default is established that the item is out and you have to take action to bring it back in. This turns out to be more effective than having the clutter as the default, and looking around your home trying to decide what to remove.

Rule of 3   Adopt the Rule of 3. Three is a cognitively magical number because our short-term memory systems are readily able to process and hold up to three chunks of information at a time. There is a reason that large numbers like 1000000000 are written as 1,000,000,000 with the commas creating groups of three zeroes; it is not an accident that children are told stories about Goldilocks and the Three Bears or the Three Blind Mice; that we divide time into past, present, and future, or that the real estate mantra is "location, location, location." Three is our mental sweet spot.

Structure and organize complexity into buckets of three wherever possible. The United States Marine Corps is structured around the Rule of 3. A corporal has a three-person fire team, a sergeant has a squad of three fire teams, a lieutenant has a platoon of three squads, and so on up to the generals. Functionally and strategically, marines are taught to condense a world of infinite possibilities into three alternative courses of action. Interestingly, the corps experimented with a Rule of 4, and effectiveness plummeted. They quickly returned to the Rule of 3.[48]

Simple Rules for a Complex World

Ants, bees, termites, and other animals are amazingly efficient, using simple rules to guide individual and group behavior. The interactions among the contributors are far more powerful than the contributions of any one individual. Their collective behavior has been named "swarm intelligence," and by studying their systems we can identify simple rules to embrace the uncertainty of our own complex world. Southwest Airlines looked to ants to help them with their cargo operations. At the time, workers were trying to load freight onto the first plane going in the needed direction, but at some airports there wasn't enough space on outbound flights to accommodate demand, while at other, less busy airports, planes were departing with empty, unused cargo space. Learning from the foraging system of ants, they devised a better allocation of resources with more efficient use of planes, slashing their need for cargo storage facilities and reducing costs. In another application, Southwest Airlines used a swarm-intelligence simulation to determine whether its open-seating policy was more efficient than the assigned seating of other airlines.[49]

One of the attributes of swarm-intelligence systems is that they are self-organizing. Southwest seating relies on passengers self-organizing once they board the plane. The adaptive ability to self-organize helped after the earthquake and tsunami that struck Japan in 2011, when rail and bus systems were suddenly halted, stranding thousands of commuters in Tokyo with no way to get home. Within hours, volunteer computer programmers created an interactive map of Tokyo to help the stranded commuters and used Twitter to broadcast a link to the tool. People quickly added information, mapping the location of makeshift shelters and those offering homes to the displaced; by midnight over 180,000 people had used the tool, sparing many the prospect of a night in the cold. The power of the tool came from the cumulative contributions of users and the intersections of their combined knowledge.[50]

An adaptive system operating with simple rules that has been successful for over 100 years plays out every workday in the densely populated and chaotic city of Mumbai. People known as *dabbawalas* deliver lunches to over 200,000 office workers throughout the city. The dabbawalas first collect the freshly cooked meals from the homes of the workers and then transport them by train, bicycle, handcart, and sometimes all three to offices and workplaces in the city. The dabba-walas have a relay system of collection regions, sorting areas, and delivery zones. One lunch may pass hands several times in the chain, yet the dabbawalas pride themselves on their impeccable on-time delivery. A very simple coding system using colors and symbols painted on each lunchbox ensures that the mostly illiterate dabbawalas can easily identify its source and destination. On average, less than one delivery in six million goes amiss. In the afternoon the process is reversed; the dabbawalas pick up and return the empty lunch boxes to the homes of their customers.

Dabbawalas take immense pride in their work and have a powerful sense of shared purpose. Delivering food on time is like serving God, and is as important as bringing medicine to the sick. To successfully navigate in the chaos of Mumbai they have self-organized into about 200 groups of 25 people each, without hierarchy or management. Each group is autonomous, giving members the flexibility to adapt to monsoons and flooding, traffic, riots, and the host of other adversities that inevitably arise. Since any delay in the chain can impact delivery down the line, each group has a few extra workers to fill in as needed. To enhance robustness further, all workers are cross-trained so each can substitute for anyone else. The dabbawalas have created an exemplary adaptive system. Companies around the world have taken note, and people like Virgin Group founder Richard Branson have visited Mumbai to learn from them.[51]

An adaptive system has three attributes:

1. Flexible—the group can quickly adapt to a changing environment
2. Robust—even when one individual falters, the group can still perform
3. Self-organized—there is little or no supervision or top-down control

For flexibility, we have to make sure that information is transparent, and is both easily and rapidly communicated in real time throughout the system.

For robustness, we need to anchor thinking with a meaningful purpose, make sure that each member has the authority to make decisions to get their job done, and that there is enough slack in the system to accommodate and recover from surprises.

Last, to be effectively self-organized, the system has to respect distributed leadership and react fluidly to independent input from every member.

Crafting the right rules to shape emergent behavior is not easy; predicting the behavior that will emerge from even two or three rules can be surprisingly difficult. Simulations and quick experiments on a small scale reveal valuable insights that can help modify rules accordingly. Most importantly, the rules must be few in number, easy to implement, and broadly applicable no matter what future unfolds.

■ ■ ■

Having an adaptive mind-set means we forever engage in rapid cycles of acting, learning, and correcting. As such, we have to learn how to cope and correct when things are not working the way we wanted. In the next chapter, we explore the emotional component of learning from error and the principles of relentless, ongoing improvement.

6

ACKNOWLEDGE, LEARN, CORRECT

FAIL FAST, FAIL EARLY, FAIL CHEAP. DON'T QUIT.

Will failure make you bitter, or will it make you better?
—John Maxwell

You can't leave a lasting footprint if you're always walking on tiptoe.
—Marion Blakey
Chair of the Federal
Aviation Administration

IN OUR QUEST TO SHAPE THE FUTURE, there will be missteps, unintended consequences, encounters with the unexpected, bad breaks, and maybe even heartbreaks. Fear of failure paralyzes many and keeps them from even starting the journey. In this chapter, we will share ideas for growing emotional resilience, developing the mind-set of practice and perseverance, and learning as a way of life.

Fear

In a television interview, Steven Spielberg was asked about an unusual painting hanging in his office. The painting is *Boy on a High Dive,* a Norman Rockwell picture of a young boy on a high diving board, lying on his stomach and clutching the board, looking down terrified.

When asked if this was his favorite Norman Rockwell painting, Spielberg said, "Well, let's put it this way: This is the Rockwell that, every time I'm ready to make a movie, every time I'm ready to commit to direct a movie, that's me—that's the feeling in my gut, before I say 'yes' to a picture. Because every movie is like looking off a three-meter diving board, every one."[1]

If Steven Spielberg, arguably one of the most successful film directors of our time, feels this way when he starts new projects, what about the rest of us when we try new things?!

The psychiatrist Dan Baker says that we have two basic fears in our lives: the fear of not having enough, and the fear of not being enough.[2] Our ancient ancestors had these fears hardwired into their thinking because they never knew when famine would strike, or even where their next meal was coming from, and never knew if they would have the strength or cunning to overcome danger in the wild. The uncertainty of survival was relentless, and the gene pool that did not have these fears couldn't last. Fear of economic scarcity pushed people to keep looking for new food sources; without the fear of not having enough, they would starve. And without the fear of not being enough, those cocky and arrogant ancestors would be beaten to a pulp by predators that were in fact stronger, faster, and better at survival.

Fear of Not Having Enough

For people today the fear of not having enough influences many decisions, sometimes dictating life choices such as professions (*My dream is to be a teacher, but I'll be an accountant because I can make more money*) and partners (*Donald is a good catch because he's rich*). The fear of not having enough can plague people no matter how much they actually have. John D. Rockefeller, at one point the world's richest man, was once asked, "How much money is enough money?" He famously replied, "Just a little bit more." Multiple Gallup Polls have asked people how much money they would need to earn to feel rich, and no matter how much they earn, people repeatedly say they would need to earn more to feel rich. The worker making $50,000 says that $100,000 a year would make him rich; but the person making $100,000 says he would need $250,000 a year to feel rich.[3]

The fear of not having enough means that most of us will never feel that we have enough money. Of course, we need enough to be able to meet our basic needs, but study after study shows that after basic needs are met, additional money is not the driver of happiness we think it is. Amassing a fortune does not create fulfillment in our lives. We have to dream bigger.

Fear of Not Being Enough

What stops us from dreaming bigger is the fear of not being enough: not smart enough, not fast enough, not attractive enough, not articulate enough—in short, the all-encompassing fear of just not being good enough to succeed. This is the fear Steven Spielberg was talking about when he explained why he has the Norman Rockwell painting in his office. This is the fear Sheryl Sandberg, COO of Facebook, described in her book exhorting women to "lean in" to their careers.[4] It's the fear that leads to stage fright for even accomplished performers: singers like Andrea Bocelli, Carly Simon, Rod Stewart, and Barbra Streisand, and actors like Sir Laurence Olivier, Jason Alexander, Robin Williams, and

Tina Fey. It's the fear that makes public speaking more dreaded than death.[5]

Imposter Syndrome

The fear of not being enough is at the heart of Imposter Syndrome. Iris first heard of this stunting affliction when she taught in an executive program for women professionals at Smith College in Massachusetts. The participants had been identified by their respective organizations as having high potential, and had been chosen to participate in a week-long executive program on leadership. Betty Shanahan, the national chair of the Society of Women Engineers, gave the keynote address during the opening dinner. After describing the program, she asked, "How many of you feel scared that you're not actually qualified to be here? That somehow you've fooled the powers-that-be to think you know what you're doing when in fact you have no idea what you're doing, and you live in fear that at some point they will figure it out?" Not only did Iris nod her own head in amazement, but almost every other head in the room was nodding as well. Everyone was shocked that others also felt this way. Betty then told the group that this feeling has a name: Imposter Syndrome. It seems to affect women more commonly then men, but men are not immune to it, either.[6] In fact, part of Imposter Syndrome is the belief that absolutely everyone else around us is as qualified as they appear to be and we are the only frauds, waiting to be discovered by the truly competent.

The problem underlying Imposter Syndrome is an all-or-nothing kind of thinking about success. It's the voice in our head that says, "If I don't know everything, then I know nothing. If I'm not perfect, then I'm incompetent." Every deficiency is seen as PPP—personal, pervasive, and permanent. You give a presentation at work, and someone critiques your conclusions. You then tell yourself, "I'm stupid [it's personal], I can't do anything right [it's pervasive], and I'll never be able to present with confidence [it's permanent]."[7]

If you suffer from Imposter Syndrome, then the great news is that you don't have to be hostage to these fears. Preset from the days of our *Homo sapiens* ancestors, our reaction to scarcity and the anxiety of not being good enough is burned in our brains, and housed in the amygdala, the highly sensitive part of our brain that specializes in fear. The excellent news is that the amygdala can be quieted; we can change our brains and learn to see ourselves differently.

We begin to change our brains, and change the impact of fear on our ability to succeed, by understanding how mind-set affects our thinking, and how thinking affects the wiring of our brains and our ability to be resilient despite fear.

The Fixed Mind-Set and the Growth Mind-Set

Stanford University professor Carol Dweck has spent her career researching achievement and success. Dweck has found that there are two fundamentally different mind-sets that impact the performance and resilience of people at any age: a fixed mind-set and a growth mind-set. In a *fixed* mind-set, people believe that the talent they are born with determines how successful they will be, and ability is something genetic that needs to be demonstrated. It is a belief that we cannot be more than we already are. In a *growth* mind-set, people believe that their abilities can be developed and improved through hard work, new experiences, and taking on challenges. Ability is dynamic and changeable. If you have a fixed mind-set, a success validates that you are smart and talented while a failure proves you are neither. In the growth mind-set, you know that talent is something you can build, and setbacks make you question your strategy, not your self-worth.

A growth mind-set does not mean that all people are born with the same inherent talents. We know playing golf or doing math is going to be easier for some people to learn. However, the idea is that everyone can get better, and we are not passive hostages to our genes or circumstances. Dweck has found that we can hold different mind-sets for specific traits. For example, you might hold a fixed mind-set for math performance and a growth mind-set for sports performance. The mind-set you hold for a particular ability will influence your behavior and motivation to persist long enough to succeed.[8]

Resilience

Bonnie St. John is an Olympic athlete who is best known for being the first African American to ever win medals in Olympic ski racing.[9] What makes Bonnie unique is that at the age of five her right leg was amputated. She had been born with a bone defect and replacing her leg with a prosthetic would give her a chance to walk. Despite this challenge, she told her mother she wanted to ski. Growing up in San Diego, California, she had the added challenge of growing up with no snow. To make matters even more difficult, her mother could not financially afford what the hobby would entail. Yet Bonnie persevered, found sponsors and scholarships, and found a way to learn to ski. She got so good that at the age of 19 she qualified to represent the USA in the 1984 Innsbruck Paralympics.

Let's go to the top of the mountain as the race is starting. In this sport, the competitors ski down two different paths, and the contestant with the fastest combined time wins the gold medal. There were 12 competitors, and after the first run down the mountain, Bonnie was in first place. You can imagine her euphoria; she said that she could already feel the gold medal hanging around her neck! Because she was in first place, she would be last to ski on the next run. This gave her an advantage because she could learn from the mistakes of those who preceded her. As she waited, she learned that everyone was falling. There was dangerous ice and a sharp curve, so when it was her turn she told herself, "Just don't fall!" She started down the mountain and successfully passed the dangers where others had fallen. Bonnie was only 300 yards from the finish line, she was 300 yards from the gold medal—and she fell. She says the anguish of having everything she had worked for end right there was almost indescribable, but the resilience she had developed in all the Olympic training forced her to get up and finish the race. Bonnie ended up with the bronze medal.

The lesson Bonnie learned that day is a lesson for all of us. Her lesson, Bonnie said, is that, "Everyone falls. Winners get back up. Gold medal winners just get up a little faster!"

Bonnie's message of resilience is powerful, but in the midst of an emotionally devastating event, it may be hard to get up, let alone recover quickly. How do gold medal winners do it?

When you were a child learning to walk, you fell down countless times and got back up. The first time you fell, you didn't give up and say, "Okay, this walking thing isn't for me. I'm obviously just a crawler." As a baby, you didn't quit; instead, you persisted, you continued learning and improving, you overcame your limitations, and eventually you became something you were not before—you became a walker.

Champion competitors say that to learn how to win, you have to first learn how to lose.

People Who Don't Know How to Lose

A person, let's call him Fred, has a fixed mind-set and believes that he has an inherited amount of given talent. For Fred, a failure is devastating because his first thought is, "I'm stupid, I can't do this, I obviously have no talent for this," so his goal is to never fail. For the fixed mind-set crowd, failures are a sign that they are not competent and not worthy. Performance mirrors ability and defines who they are, and so they always have to look good. Managing their image is a priority.

An adult like Fred is afraid of being judged by others, even as he constantly judges himself. Faced with a challenge, the little voice in his head says "Uh-oh, what if I screw up? People will know I'm not as smart as they think I am. Maybe I'm not as smart as I want to be. Better not try this." Every setback puts a dent in their self-esteem, so they shy away from stretch goals and if something isn't working, they give up right away. If they can't win easily, they don't want to play.

Fred-types believe that not only do they have to be perfect to prove how talented they are, but that success has to come easily. The ease of achieving success validates their talent. If Jenny next door has to practice, study, or prepare for days while Fred aces a performance test with no practice, study, or preparation, Fred concludes that he is smarter and more talented. Dweck does not argue that we are all born with the same talents and that any one of us can become an Olympic-gold-medalist, Nobel-prize-winning, Hall-of-Fame superstar if we just put our minds to it. What her research shows is that people with fixed mind-sets give up the minute something is difficult. They never give themselves the chance to see how far they can go or how high they can climb, and they will never know how good they can become.

A growth mind-set is the attitude that talent or ability can be built. Persistence, effort, practice, and strategy play a huge role in shaping success, and these are factors we can control. A person with this mind-set sees a world of opportunity. Failure is disappointing, we don't like it, but it is perceived as useful information, a signal that we need to try a different tactic. It's feedback, albeit perhaps an uncomfortable learning experience, that tells us something we didn't know but that we can use to get better.

What is the response to failure in the two mind-sets? In the fixed mind-set, the response is, "I can't do this." In the growth mind-set, the response is, "I can't do this—yet."

Is there a way to change a mind-set, to reshape a fixed mind-set into a growth mind-set? Thankfully, yes!

"Life Isn't About Finding Yourself. Life Is About Creating Yourself."[10]

Studies have shown that mind-sets can shift, no matter how old we are. Researchers have worked with children, athletes, and managers to create profound attitude changes with surprisingly simple and brief interventions.[11]

For example, Dweck worked with fifth-grade children with a fixed mind-set; these were the kids who avoided challenging assignments, didn't do their homework, and goofed off in class. Their test scores were low and they called themselves "stupid." She also worked with the Blackburn Rovers, a British professional soccer team whose athletes believed that talent was all that mattered, that star players are born, not made. The coach asked her to help because many of the athletes were not reaching their potential. Unlike the students, the athletes didn't think they lacked talent; they believed that their exceptional talent was all they needed.[12] Both the children and the athletes were operating from fixed mind-set beliefs about their inherent talents, stunting their potential to improve.

Peter Heslin and his colleagues studied managers who judged both themselves and their employees through the limiting frame of a fixed mind-set.[13] These bosses didn't notice improvement in their workers; their first impressions were permanent. They didn't mentor their employees, as they believed people were either naturals or not. These managers also could not tolerate criticism of their own work. They felt that because they were in a high-status position, that they had to have all the answers and that failure would tarnish their image.

In a few short workshop sessions people in all of these groups— the children, the athletes, and the managers—experienced a shift from a fixed mind-set to a growth mind-set. The fixed mind-set is grounded in antiquated beliefs about the brain. Not long ago scientists believed that the brain is preset and that we are born with all the brain power we will ever have. The latest neuroscience research has debunked this belief and shown that our brains are remarkably flexible. As we learned previously, every experience we have grows and changes our brain, every day of our lives. These groups of fixed mind-set people were taught what we will explain in the next few pages and were able to dramatically change their outlook and their behavior. In the following sections, we discuss how any one of us can develop a stronger growth mind-set.

Use Your Mind to Change Your Brain

How does the brain change? We are born with billions of brain cells, but at birth they haven't really done much yet. As we noted in Chapter 3, "Galvanize Your Team," each brain cell has the ability to form connections with other brain cells, resulting in trillions of connections. Every experience creates new connections in the brain. Reading these sentences right now, and learning about the two types of mind-sets, is creating new connections in your brain. It's almost startling to think that the physical structure of your brain is changing all the time based on how you use your mind. How much does it change? As described in Chapter 3, 2 of the 3 pounds of your adult brain are connections between cells that are formed based on your experiences. This shaping never ends, and we continue to grow connections with everything we learn. Our brains grow stronger and better with use.[14]

Heslin and his colleagues taught the fixed mind-set groups of managers about the brain and then asked them to think about examples from their lives that demonstrated growth. For example, they were asked, "What are some things you thought you could never do, and then you did them?" They were also asked to write a note to someone they knew who was struggling, and offer advice about what they could do to develop and improve. As a result of the workshops, participants became more open to the opportunity for growth. Managers became more sensitive to detecting improvement in employees, became better mentors, and even became more open to critical feedback on their own performance. Likewise, through Dweck's work with the fifth graders, teachers reported that the students became more diligent and worked harder to improve; by the end of the term, the jump in their math grades meant that they had challenged themselves to learn difficult concepts. The coach of the Blackburn Rangers saw great promise in the approach, too, and is using the workshop methods starting with the newest recruits each year.[15] The effects of these efforts were lasting.

Business organizations with a fixed mind-set don't allow people to learn through quick experiments; their employee development programs are nonexistent because they have hired "talent," senior leadership doesn't see any reason to invest in their own development, and the core message is "don't mess up." The United States Olympic Committee, coordinating the NBA-studded basketball teams that represented Team USA, was mired in this mind-set before Coach K took over. Players were given almost no time to practice together, because it was assumed that they did not need it. Talent was enough. When talent alone resulted in a bronze medal in 2004, Coach K brought the growth mind-set to the organization, created a system for success, and turned things around. Olympic organizers with the fixed mind-set sent talent out to the court to demonstrate their ability; by contrast, Coach K, with his growth mind-set, used meetings and practices to develop the team.

Facing Difficult Situations

Even with a growth mind-set, facing failure, or even the prospect of failing, is not easy for people. It can range from uncomfortable to paralyzing.

We are constantly running a narrative in our heads, explaining the world to ourselves. When something doesn't work the way we wanted it to, when we do something we now wish we hadn't done, when we don't live up to our standards, there are four possible ways to think about it. Three of these ways involve internal dialogue that results in toxic levels of negative emotions and stunts growth. The fourth way of thinking helps us frame events in a way that enhances resilience and promotes our ability to handle the rough and the tough. We will start with the three ways of thinking that limit our ability to recover in the face of difficulty.[16]

Catastrophic Thinking

In catastrophic thinking, every negative outcome is believed to be so devastatingly awful that recovery is impossible. Even the smallest distress is amplified into horrible shock. Another term to describe this thinking is "awfulizing." For example, imagine you are sitting in a plush lobby, waiting to be interviewed for a job that you really want. The voice in your head might provoke you with thoughts like, "What if they ask me something I don't know? What if I say something stupid?" These questions by themselves are not catastrophic. What will make them catastrophic is the answer you give yourself. With awfulizing, your response to "What if they ask me something I don't know?" might sound like this: "They will think I'm an idiot . . . they'll think I am totally unqualified for this position! This is my worst nightmare. . . . I hate my life. . . . I can't stand this. . . . I'm never going to get a good job. . . . I have a mortgage to pay. . . . I'm going to end up homeless!" By awfulizing the possibility that you may not know an answer to one of their questions, you end up living on the streets!

How often do you awfulize about something, and by the time it actually happens it's not nearly as bad as all the awfulizing you did? It could be a difficult conversation you don't want to have with someone, or an event you don't want to go to, or any other future you anticipate with dread that turns out to be excessive. This type of thinking makes you incredibly anxious and stressed, and prevents you from thinking clearly about how to handle a situation effectively.

Absolutist Thinking

Absolutist thinking starts when people confront situations that don't conform to their opinion of what ought to happen. This is a "must, have to, can't, should" kind of thinking in which we berate ourselves for not being enough. For example, back in the lobby for the job interview, in addition to awfulizing, your internal dialogue might continue with, "I should have reviewed their financial report last night instead of watching TV. . . . Why didn't I think to bring hard copies of my letters of recommendation? . . . I have to outshine the other candidates and get this job. . . . I can't screw this up!" In the words of our colleague Art Lange, "we're 'shoulding' all over ourselves!"

Other forms of absolutist thinking come in terms of "always," "every," and "never." When we think in rigid categories of all or nothing, we take a single incident and use it to define the whole. If you fail to get the job offer, you conclude, "I'll never find a job." If you don't do well on a math test, you decide, "I can't do math." If you stumble in a presentation, you tell yourself, "I always screw up important meetings." We take isolated events and overgeneralize them in our thinking into a never-ending pattern that is out of our control to change.

Denial and Rationalization

The third kind of maladaptive thinking is denial. We add disclaimers to our efforts that actually, if things don't turn out well, we didn't care that much to begin with. With this kind of cover-up, we can dismiss a failure and downplay the outcome. The problem is that we are lying to ourselves; these are things we actually do care about, but to keep ourselves from feeling bad, we try to talk ourselves out of feeling anything at all. Let's go back to our interview example. Suppose you find out one week later that you didn't get the job. Denial dialogue might include rationalizations like, "Whatever. . . . Interviews are so fake anyway. . . . They asked some really stupid questions. . . . Some of those guys were so arrogant, who wants to work for people like that? . . . If they can't see what I have to offer they can't be a very smart company. . . . I would really rather have a job closer to home. . . ."

Denial is a weak attempt to boost our self-image by minimizing the situation. We disengage and distance ourselves from our commitment or interest. The problem is that we actually do care, and if we were able to digest the situation in a more balanced way, we could learn from it and handle future interviews more effectively. Denial shuts down any such learning and growth.[17]

Constructive Comebacks

Challenging maladaptive thinking is the first step in thinking for growth. Cognitive behavioral psychologists call this "erasing and replacing." When you recognize any of the three negative types of thinking starting to unfold in your internal dialogue, you consciously catch yourself and say "STOP." This can be difficult in the heat of the moment, especially since many of our thoughts occur automatically—you have so much practice with the negative kinds of thinking that they happen without much awareness. In a difficult situation, it can help to just ask yourself, "Am I using any dysfunctional thinking? Am I awfulizing? Am I shoulding? Am I denying?"

Once you catch yourself, the next step is to dispute the assumptions underlying the maladaptive thinking. Strategies for questioning assumptions include evaluating the evidence that supports or contradicts your thinking, and expanding your thinking to include at least one other possible way of assessing the situation. To see this kind of thinking in action, let's revisit the job interview one more time. Sitting in the lobby, you started awfulizing about a question you may not be able to answer. You catch yourself turning this potential event into a catastrophe so you stop yourself. You can then say:

Realistically, there may be questions that I don't know the answer to. I don't like when it happens, but when people have asked me questions in the past and I didn't know the answer, what did I do? Has it ever turned out okay? My best responses were always to tell the truth, say that I don't know, but to also tell them that I have some ideas related to their question and if it's possible, that I know what to do to find the correct answer to their question. I would really prefer to be able to answer every question. But even if I can't, I can show them what I do when I don't know something and I can still have an intelligent conversation.

Notice, you are not telling yourself that everything will work out perfectly and that you can answer every question. To the contrary, you are facing the reality that failure to answer a question is an option, and it's an outcome from which you can recover.

If you start shoulding on yourself ("I have to calm down!"), catch yourself berating yourself and STOP. Replace it with constructive thinking—"It's normal to be nervous before an interview. I'm going to take a few deep breaths and think how to channel this case of the jitters into a way to show them that I am excited to be here."

And if you don't get the job, and find yourself denying that it matters at all, it's important to remember that feeling sad or disappointed is part of life. A constructive thought would be, "I'm disappointed and even embarrassed that I didn't get the offer. This was a frustrating experience and I am committed to finding a way to present myself more effectively in the future. . . . I'll start by talking to a few friends and asking them what they do to prepare for interviews."

To build on the quote that started this chapter, will you allow failure to make you bitter, will you say "Why bother?" or will you use failure to make yourself better?

Healthy Negative Emotion

People mistakenly worry that restructuring thinking with constructive comebacks is designed to eliminate all negative emotion. Part of the problem with awfulizing and shoulding is that they trigger *excessive* anxiety, fear, anger, and guilt. These damaging levels of emotion undermine our ability to effectively handle difficult situations. Denial is a form of self-preservation to shield us from these excessive feelings so we don't let ourselves feel anything at all.

In contrast, constructive comebacks replace excessive and toxic levels of negative emotion with uncomfortable but not debilitating negative emotions. Instead of destructive anxiety we frame our thoughts to feel constructive concern. Instead of destructive rage we frame our thoughts to feel constructive annoyance. It's okay to be concerned, annoyed, sad, disappointed, or remorseful. These emotions motivate us to think about ways to improve for the future. Constructive comebacks, then, don't eliminate all negative emotion; they reframe our thinking to feel the kind of negative emotion that can help us recover from failure and shape future success.

Putting names to emotions isn't easy and most of us have a very limited vocabulary for naming our feelings. People use an average of five to seven words to describe their entire emotional field. These are usually variants on feeling glad, sad, bad, or mad. Having the right label for an emotion allows you to experience it more fully and appropriately. Take *mad*, for example. It can mean exasperated, irked, annoyed, bitter, hostile, outraged, frustrated, confused, disappointed, and more. Each is a unique emotion and using the right label can actually change what you experience. Putting our feelings into words—the right words—can help us harness our emotions more appropriately and handle situations more effectively.[18]

Personal Defeat

One of Iris's daughters is passionate about musical theater. By first grade she knew entire shows by heart and would enlist her sisters to create living room performances of *Fiddler on the Roof* and *Oklahoma!*, complete with makeup, costumes, and props. At her insistence, the family attended every musical put on yearly by the neighborhood high school.

Iris's daughter could not wait for the day that she, too, might sing on the high school stage. When she finally got to high school she learned that there was an unofficial rule about who would be cast in the shows. Lead roles were strictly for seniors, and the youngest students could at best be extras. As a freshman she decided to audition anyway, and was thrilled when she landed a small part. The next year, she was cast in a larger role. As a junior she was in a major role, and then came the excitement of senior year.

After the general auditions for the lead female role, two names were announced for the callback finals: Iris's daughter and a junior. The lead had never gone to a junior so everyone—her daughter, friends, and even other teachers—were sure of the outcome. Late Friday afternoon the cast was announced. The lead role had been given to the junior.

Her daughter came home immediately, devastated and humiliated, and locked herself in her room. Concerned and wanting to help, Iris weighed her options. One possibility would be to go in and commiserate with her daughter, decrying the injustice and demeaning the judgment of the casting teacher ("How awful, how dare she, what's wrong with her!"). This option would only fuel the anger her daughter was already feeling, so she did not want to take that path. Another option would be to go in and try to reason with her, to help her put it into perspective ("Oh honey, I know it feels bad, but you're graduating and going to college and you have your whole life ahead of you . . ."). This tactic would essentially be denying the depth of her daughter's pain, and her response would justifiably be a rendition of, "Please go away, you just don't understand!" So, neither of these options would be helpful.

In that moment of parental helplessness, a third possibility came to mind. Iris took a blank piece of paper and a black pen, and drew the picture below:

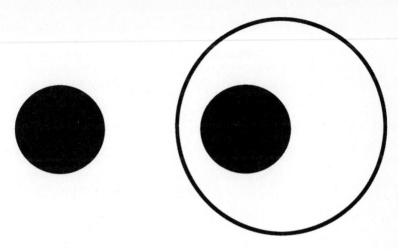

Figure 6.1   What Is the Size of Your Universe?

She took the page to her daughter's room and, putting it in front of her, said, "You don't have to say anything. I know it feels horrible. Right now your entire universe feels like this black dot on the left. What happened isn't going to change. The only thing you can control is how you look at it. You can decide that your universe is the black dot on the left, or you can decide that your universe is the circle on the right. The black dot is one part of that universe, but it's a bigger universe."

Without pressing any further, she gave her the page and left the room. It didn't take long; within about half an hour her daughter came downstairs, disappointed but no longer crushed, and announced that she would accept the secondary role that she had been offered.

What had Iris's daughter done? She had filled in the larger circle herself, with things in her life that were meaningful to her. She had found her own way of putting the loss in context. None of us wants to be miserable, but sometimes we need help seeing the bigger universe. Remember that you can't show people their unique universe; they have to find it themselves. What you can do is provide the tools that make the discovery easier.

Organizational Defeat

Entire organizations can feel the crush of defeat, but it is their perspective and response to failure that determines their future, not the defeat itself. One of the best-known business failures in history was the Ford Edsel. Its introduction was a carefully planned, thoughtfully designed maneuver to capture the upper middle class market segment. Its abject failure could have been attributed to stupid consumers ("How awful, how dare they, what's wrong with them!") or brushed off with denial and rationalizations ("All our other cars are huge successes, this is an anomaly, it's just one of those things, you can't win all the time. . .") but instead Ford opted to question its own perception of the universe. They visited the world of the customer and realized that their views of customer segmentation based on economic status were no longer valid. The year was 1957 and demographics were shifting; values were changing and the 1960s were about to profoundly change the American social fabric. The failure of the Edsel was the first sign to Ford that something was afoot, and by choosing to question, they discovered that a lifestyle differentiation was emerging. This led to Ford's redesign of the Thunderbird and then the debut of the Mustang, successes that dramatically impacted Ford's competitive advantage.

For each of us personally, for teams, and for organizations, *we're not finished when we fail; we're only finished when we quit*. An alternative to ignoring failure is to foster an environment that systematically studies it and an attitude of relentless ongoing improvement.

10,000 Hours

In a growth mind-set, we know we have to take action to develop our abilities, as in the old joke—a young girl stops a policeman in New York City and asks, "How do you get to Carnegie Hall?" He tells her, "Practice, kid!"

But what about Mozart? His name often comes up as an example of pure innate talent, a genius in diapers who changed the world of music. Dig a little deeper, and we find that Mozart worked long and hard before he became "Mozart." Mozart the child was tutored by his father, a professional musician himself. One of the key findings in many instances of the child prodigy is that a dedicated parent nurtured their interest from a very early age. True, Mozart's first piano concertos were written when he was 11 and 16 years old, but they contain no original music. They are variations on the music of other composers. This may have been his father's way of creating a deliberate practice opportunity; Mozart could use existing pieces to practice writing for groups of instruments. Many of his earliest works that do contain original music have been pretty much ignored by the music world because they weren't all that good. So Mozart started his career like many aspiring musicians, producing music that for all practical purposes needed more work. His masterful pieces only started to emerge after about 10 years of dedicated, deliberate practice to develop his unique sound.

Mozart's path is repeated in multiple domains where we find extraordinary achievements of an individual.[19] Picasso didn't just pick up a brush in preschool and produce museum-quality paintings. He, too, had a father who nurtured him. Picasso's father was an art teacher and painter; Picasso went to art school and his early works show deliberate practice drawing the human body in tricky poses. The paintings that we now instantly think of when we hear his name did not emerge until more than 10 years into his career. In sports, athletes such as Tiger Woods and Michael Phelps were also nurtured and trained from a very young age, practicing for hours to develop their unique styles. Ditto for Bobby Fischer, the renowned chess champion. Fischer started playing at the age of six when he and his sister bought a toy chess set at a candy store. His sister lost interest, but Bobby began to study the game intensely, and by the age of eight he found the coaching he needed in the Brooklyn Chess Club. At the age of 15, Fischer became a grandmaster, the game's highest designation of expertise; the next year, he dropped out of school because classes took him away from his focus on the game.[20]

Investigation of just about any phenomenal success story reveals people who practiced and perfected their skills over many years. They became experts in their domain because of their dedicated and relentless efforts to improve themselves until they reached the top of their field. Interestingly, record-breaking levels of achievement are first reached by a single standout individual. Within a short time others in the field are able to design training and practice strategies that allow them to also attain this level, and eventually it becomes the domain standard. Many records set in Olympic Games of the past are now standard levels of performance for college athletes and even committed high school amateurs. Beating the 4-minute mile in running, performing the triple axel in ice skating, or a double somersault in diving are but a few examples of previously impossible maneuvers that have become expected by any respected athlete in the respective sport. The exceptionally dedicated relentlessly fine-tune their training strategies to make impossibilities possible.

Research on expertise concludes that consistent extraordinary achievement depends on a foundation of extensive experience, and that many thousands of hours of specific types of practice are necessary to shape the highest levels of success. The growth of expertise and success has been investigated in a wide span of domains including computer programming, firefighting, surgery, writing and many others, but the pattern is the same for all. Deliberate practice over an average of 10,000 hours is the way to push out into the extreme of the distribution curve, and to move into the ranks of the exceptional.[21]

This brings us to a potential misunderstanding we need to clear up. In his book *Outliers*, Malcolm Gladwell popularized the idea of the alluring and magical formula of 10,000 hours of practice to achieve expertise.[22] Many people latched on to the number. However, just logging in and racking up hours in any field is going to do very little to move anyone's talent and skill set into the domain of the exceptional, even after 10,000 hours. Years of driving (totaling more than 10,000 hours) have not turned you into a professional race car driver. More than 10,000 hours of cooking family meals has not turned anyone we know into a Top Chef. Expertise does not come about from just raw *amount* of practice; the *quality* of the practice is a key factor that determines ultimate levels of success.

How You Practice Matters

Not all practice is equally effective and noted researchers—Anders Ericsson from Florida State University, and our colleagues, Robert Bjork and Elizabeth Bjork from UCLA—have done extensive research to identify the features of smart practice. Ericsson recommends a process he describes as "deliberate practice," and the Bjorks' research shows the advantage of practice that includes "desirable difficulties" that support comprehension, learning, remembering, and long-term performance.[23]

Deliberate Practice and Desirable Difficulties

"Deliberate practice" is the term Ericsson uses to describe a persistent pursuit of new challenges with a focus on finding our weaknesses, identifying errors, and inventing ways to overcome them. It requires the kind of effort that is all encompassing—physical, cognitive, and emotional. Instead of idly practicing the skills that come easily, we root out our flaws and fix them, using mindful and evidence-driven practice strategies. These strategies are not necessarily enjoyable, introducing what the Bjorks term "desirable difficulties," but they differentiate the exceptional outcomes from the great.

As an example, advanced-level piano students at the University of Texas–Austin were studied as they practiced a difficult piano piece.[24] They were then ranked according to the quality of their final performance. The researchers looked back at the practice sessions to search for differentiating factors between students who gave the top performances and those who gave the lesser ones. The most critical factor separating the students was *not* related to the length or frequency of their practice, but rather how they dealt with errors while they practiced. The most remarkable pianists were those who caught each error while practicing, deliberately and intently worked to make it right, and only then continued with the piece. These top students did not make fewer errors at the start of their practice sessions; what they did was handle their errors strategically. Instead of quickly fixing a mistake and moving on, or glossing over it assuming it was an anomaly, the top performers interrupted their progress through the piece to work on their fingering, reevaluated what they were doing, tried several ways to approach that part of the piece before settling on the one that worked best, and only then moved on.

More broadly, then, what is deliberate practice? It is a sustained focus on what you are not doing well with strategies designed to improve your skills or understanding. Elite experts bring deliberate thinking into their practice sessions, with enhanced concentration and undivided attention dedicated to the task. Rote or mindless repetitions do not enhance performance. Recent brain studies corroborate this difference in performance, showing brain growth as a function of the type of repetition used. Imagine we were to look at the brain of a violinist. The area of their brain dedicated to the movement of the fingers controlling the strings would be larger than that of people who do not play any stringed instrument.[25] Similar results have been found in the brains of London taxi drivers, who train for three to four years to learn the routes of the city. Researchers studied their brains before and after this long period of training; those who qualified to pass the rigorous test showing they had learned the city streets also showed significant increased growth in the posterior hippocampus, the part of the brain dedicated to memory.[26] Both professional musicians and the London taxi drivers show a change in brain structure after repeated deliberate practice. Our brains dedicate more neural real estate to functions based on our performance demands.

Now, suppose we were to go every night to the home of a person who does not play the violin, and while they are asleep, we move their fingers over a violin as though they are playing. Their fingers would be going through the same physical motions, for the same amount of time as a musician would consciously move them, but their minds would not be involved. Despite the physical activity, their brain would look just like the brain of someone who does not play at all. Mental engagement must accompany the physical activity for the brain to grow and for performance to improve.[27]

Ericsson quotes a violin maestro who asked his professor how many hours to practice every day.[28] He reportedly replied, "It really doesn't matter how long. If you practice with your fingers, no amount is enough. If you practice with your head, two hours is plenty." While two hours may not seem like much, the concentration and mental effort required is cognitively exhausting, and can't be continued indefinitely.

Making It Difficult Is Good for You

Deliberate practice is most effective when desirable difficulties are interwoven into the process. Why would you purposely set yourself up to fail and make your practice more demanding? It seems counterintuitive to set yourself up for failure. And yet, optimizing the effectiveness of practice for learning, growth, and subsequent success requires exactly that: designing challenging, *desirable failures* into the process. Practice conditions that result in rapid performance success in the short term often fail to have long-term lasting impact. In contrast, challenging practice conditions that can be grueling, require undivided attention, often feel self-defeating, push you out of your comfort zones, and feel slow are the keys to advancing long-term learning and success. This is true across all domains of learning, not just for motor skill development but also cognitive, social, and emotional development.

Desirable Difficulties in Practice

Dan McLaughlin, a professional photographer, decided in April 2010 to quit his job and to dedicate 10,000 hours to learn to play golf. He set a goal to get so good that he could qualify to compete in the PGA tour. This sounded insane to his friends, since in his entire life up to this point he had only swung at a few golf balls, and not very well at that. Not an especially athletic guy, Dan had no particular advantage starting this journey that he hoped would propel him into the ranks of professional golfers. But his was not going to be the typical approach to learning the sport.

At first he thought he could dedicate 10 hours a day to practice, and be done with his 10,000 hours in less than four years. However, Dan met with Professor Ericsson, who explained that deliberate practice could not be crammed into an intensive massed numbers of hours. The concentration and desirable difficulties that define deliberate practice and shape long-term success require that practice be distributed in shorter sessions over more time. A typical day for Dan would involve four to six hours of practice, and only time that he spent mindfully engaged with the ball would count toward his 10,000 hours.

Ericsson points out that all golfers start out as novices, having to constantly recheck their grip on the club, think through every movement of the swing, assess how hard to hit the ball, adjust their posture as they try to hit the ball (and try not to fling chunks of grass in the air!)—in short, the novice has to concentrate heavily. Eventually it starts to feel familiar (Ericsson says it takes about 50 hours) and the novice becomes able to hit the ball pretty decently. With a little more practice, strokes become more automatic, requiring less concentration and less focus on every muscle and movement. At this point, players often plateau. They start to practice only the things that are easy for them, or they start playing golf as a social game. And this is where improvement ends.

Ericsson essentially warned Dan that playing a social game of golf—chatting with buddies, briefly looking at the ball before a swing, having relaxed fun on the golf course—would not improve his game in any substantive way. Deliberate practice would be grueling and would include lots of self-imposed, purposeful opportunities to fail. Like the advanced piano students, Dan's response to these assorted failures would be a key element in honing the skills needed to achieve expertise.[29]

Dan also consulted with UCLA professor Robert Bjork, who confirmed Ericsson's recommendations for practice, and elaborated on the idea of creating opportunities to fail by incorporating desirable difficulties into his program.[30] Desirable difficulties are strategies that might appear to impede progress during training, but ultimately yield greater long-term benefits than equivalent time spent on easier practice routines. The approach is to identify a weakness that you want to improve and then incorporate short challenges that are not too easy, nor so difficult to the point of giving up. Making a practice session too rote and easy may create an immediate sense of success in the short term, but the learning will not be long lived. If you have ever crammed for an exam by pulling an all-nighter you know the drill. Your immediate performance on the exam the next day may be enough to help you pass the class, but shortly thereafter you probably remember next to nothing. Rereading a chapter three times produces incrementally diminishing returns in a single study block.

Instead, to integrate information into long-term memory, you would be much better off with a few desirable difficulties. Desirable difficulties promote a deeper processing of material resulting in the storage of a stronger, more accessible memory that can be drawn upon more readily later, even after time erodes accessibility to weaker memories.

Desirable difficulties that challenge us in effective ways include spacing instead of massed repetition, varying the practice conditions, interleaving related skills, and using tests as learning events. Let's look at how you can put these strategies into practice.

Space Repetitions Don't study in a single block of time. If you are going to review material three times, space your study sessions across three different blocks of time. Suppose you are learning a piano piece, and you want to practice it this week. You could practice for a solid hour on Sunday, or you could practice for 20 minutes on Sunday, another 20 minutes on Tuesday, and another 20 minutes on Friday. Most people think dedicating an hour sounds more serious and feels intuitively more effective, but research consistently shows that spacing the repetitions is much better for long-term successful performance.[31]

A possible reason for enhanced learning with spacing is that it forces you to reactivate your memory. If you do A and then do A right away again, A is still activated and no reloading is necessary. With the passage of time, the memory for how to do A has to be reactivated from scratch. Repeated reactivations during study engage the same processes you will have to generate later when you need access to the memory and have to reload it from an inactive state.

From a practical standpoint, how should you space the intervals between repetitions? The optimal schedule is to create expanding intervals rather than equally spaced intervals. Why insert more time between progressive repetitions? With repeated practice the information becomes better learned and it takes longer to become inactive. The greatest impact of a subsequent repetition occurs when information is on the edge of inaccessibility.

A robust finding across scores of studies shows that increasingly longer lags between repetitions leads to better long-term learning and recall accessibility of information. As a practical example, Iris took a CPR class on a Friday afternoon and didn't want to forget what she had learned. Over the next week she reviewed the content and spaced the repetitions. She went over the steps on the drive home after the class (about 1 hour after the lesson), repeated it the next morning (about 12 hours later), then two days later on Monday, followed by two more repetitions—on Friday (four days later) and finally the following Friday (one week later). So the intervals between repetitions expanded from 1 hour, to 12 hours, to two days, four days, and seven days. In the future, if she ever needs this information, she is more likely to be able to reactivate the steps of CPR than had she done all five repetitions on the drive home.

Leverage Context   Consider the context in which you will need to access the material from memory in the future. If you know exactly where you will need the information (e.g., you are an emergency room doctor and you need to learn techniques for your job), then study the information in a context as similar as possible to the context you will be in when you will need to recall the information. Will there be noise, tumult, and lots of people around you in the medical emergency of the future? Bring that future to the present and incorporate it into your study environment. If you can't actually study in the emergency room, or physically create a simulation, then use your imagination. Create the future context in your mind's eye during study. If you are preparing a speech and you know where you will be giving it, simulate that context by either practicing in the presentation room or pretending you are there in your imagination as you review the points of your talk.

For most situations, when we acquire knowledge we don't know in what future context we will need to access those memories. Here the optimal way to rehearse is to mix it up; study in a variety of contexts. When Iris took the CPR class she wanted to review the steps a few times. Hopefully she will never need to apply CPR, but if she does there is no way to know in advance what the environment will be. To maximize future access to this knowledge, Iris reviewed the procedure in her kitchen, at work, in the supermarket, in the car, and on a walk in her neighborhood. Five repetitions of the material, in five different contexts, makes future retrieval more likely than had she repeated it five times in the same context.[32]

Interleave Practice with Related Skills   Interleaving related skills adds a beneficial layer of complexity to the study phase. Instead of blocking your practice by focusing repeatedly on one task, and then moving on to the next task, interleaving means mixing in a variety of related tasks within a single block. For example, suppose you are learning a foreign language, and to practice saying sentences in the past, present, and future tense, you plan to study for 45 minutes. Instead of separating the tenses into three 15-minute blocks for past, present, and future, you are much better off interleaving the tenses across the 45 minutes.

An impressive demonstration of interleaving practice was conducted with children.[33] The kids practiced throwing a beanbag at a target on the floor. Half of the children practiced at a single fixed distance (4 feet away) while the other half practiced at varied distances (3 and 5 feet away). After a delay, all the kids were tested at the distance used in the fixed-practice condition (4 feet away). You probably expect that the kids who practiced from the tested distance would do best, but the opposite was true. Somehow the effect of varied practice, even when the tested distance was not included in the variations, outweighed the benefit of practicing at the tested distance.

The same benefits of interleaving have been shown for adults and for more complex material than throwing beanbags.[34] Imagine being in an art appreciation class and having to learn the styles of different artists. Traditional teaching methods would approach the works of each artist separately so as not to confuse the learners. In a fascinating study, participants were tasked with learning the styles of 12 artists based on a viewing of six sample paintings per artist. In the experiment, half the learners got the paintings in blocks as they would be presented in the typical classroom. ("Here are six paintings by Picasso. Now that you have learned Picasso, let's move on to Miró . . ."). The other half of the learners studied the paintings in a randomized fashion, with any given artist's paintings interwoven among those of the other artists. When all participants were later shown a series of new paintings (paintings by these artists that they had not seen during the learning phase) and were asked to identify the artist, the group that viewed the interwoven learning set was much better at identifying the correct artist.[35] This flies in the face of our intuitive sense of how to learn, but it aligns beautifully with the underlying reasons for the benefits of spacing discussed earlier. The massed, consecutive presentation of the work of a single artist doesn't create the same cognitive demand as the presentation of randomized works. When you see a Picasso, then a Miró, then see a Picasso again, you have to reactivate and reload your Picasso memory.

As we saw with these examples, we are finding more and more evidence that reactivating and reloading are fundamental to enhancing learning that readies us for novel situations.

Retrieve to Remember Testing yourself while learning isn't just a way to measure progress; it turns out to be a terrific learning strategy.[36] Retrieval, in the words of Robert Bjork, is a powerful memory modifier. When information is successfully accessed from memory, it changes the nature of what is stored, making it more recallable in the future. The gain from testing is often greater than restudying or an additional presentation of the material. Tests, then, turn out to be powerful learning events to enhance long-term access to information. Not only is the information trace in memory getting stronger, but we are also gaining *retrieval practice*, engaging in the processes that we will have to rely on in the future.

But what happens if you can't answer a test question correctly? Does producing a wrong answer somehow weaken or corrupt the correct answer in memory? What if you produce no answer at all? In the first case, you thought you were right but you were wrong. In the second case, you discover you don't have the answer. Astonishingly, even an unsuccessful recall attempt makes a subsequent recall more likely to succeed! It appears that recall failure changes the nature of what is stored, but in a positive way—it makes it more likely for the correct answer to be accessible later—provided you get feedback to learn from your mistake. If you struggle to recall something and finally Google the answer, or if you generate a wrong answer and get feedback with the correct answer, you will remember the correct information more successfully than if you don't try to generate the information at all.[37] When Iris was reviewing the steps of CPR, she knew she had 18 facts to recall. If she couldn't remember one of them, she tried for a while, but if that didn't help, she eventually looked it up in the booklet she had been given. Interestingly, the next time Iris reviewed the material, those facts were the easiest to recall. We can look at this as another example of desirable failure that promotes future success.

Shaping Practice to Shape Success

The goal of any practice is to shape success for the moments when it matters. By integrating these strategies into training, it makes the practice harder, but the ultimate performance (when it counts) more likely to succeed. It would certainly have been easier for Iris to review the steps of CPR during her short drive home, without spacing, and without moving to different contexts, and by the fifth run through the material in the car she would have been able to articulate the steps with little effort. Like many students, she could have been lulled into thinking that she now knew CPR based on how easily the information came to her as she pulled into the garage. But even perfect performance during practice can be short lived and lead to performance defeat when it actually matters. This kind of perfect performance is like a mirage in the desert; it looks like real learning but quickly vanishes. Practice sessions have to be designed for durability and robustness, incorporating learning strategies known to enhance long-term performance success.

Depending on the skill set under development, a practice program must be tailored to optimally shape success. For athletes, firefighters, military personnel, pilots, surgeons, musicians, and others who need to learn a complex choreography of skills, there can actually be great advantage to starting with a practice routine that first leads to rapid performance success within the practice session. Massed repetitions focused on one task, all in the same learning context, with lots of feedback from a coach or teacher, helps to create initial fluency. Once the skill feels familiar, this would be the time to introduce conditions of desirable difficulties, to ensure that performance success is sustainable.[38]

Many organizations across a wide range of industries have created rotational leadership-development programs, essentially integrating desirable difficulties into the initial training of new hires. In organizations as diverse as Ford, Amazon, Johnson & Johnson, Starbucks, Raytheon, and even the FBI, new hires rotate across multiple business units and functions, to gain experience and learn the breadth and variety of required skills necessary to develop as leaders. Typically lasting for two years, the new hire spends a few months in each functional area. These programs incorporate the advantages we saw from the spacing of repetitions, change in context, interweaving of related skills, and retrieval practice so critical to long-term performance success.

Creating the "Culture of ROI": Relentless Ongoing Improvement

In 1919, the Eighteenth Amendment to the U.S. Constitution established Prohibition, banning the manufacture and sale of alcohol. In 1933, the Twenty-First Amendment acknowledged the error, repealing Prohibition. It is an excellent lesson to us all that the Eighteenth Amendment was neither replaced nor erased. It is a permanent reminder that we need to be open to new facts, open to change, and relentlessly seeking to improve.

Just as Dan McLaughlin wants to become a world-class golfer, and legislators enact laws with the goal of improving society, organizations with a growth mind-set constantly question how to better serve their purpose. They want to develop new products, services, strategies, and tactics to get better all the time. In their quest to relentlessly improve themselves, they know that some ideas will work out better than others, and some ideas will fail. Giving people license to explore and try new ideas, and creating an environment of amnesty when ideas don't work, is key in a culture of relentless ongoing improvement.

Upon hearing this, some managers worry that creating an environment that tolerates (or even encourages!) learning from errors will lead to an "anything goes" attitude and a sloppy work ethic. Indeed, encouraging any and all sorts of failure would be at the very least silly, and potentially even disastrous. Nobody should wake up in the morning, eagerly looking forward to angering customers or misdiagnosing patients. Just as we want to incorporate *desirable difficulties* to improve human performance, we should aim to promote the *desirable failures* that improve organizational performance in the pursuit of purpose. Acknowledging and learning from failure is a necessary element of the system for shaping success, and not a license to abandon accountability. We give people the responsibility to ultimately get it right when it matters, by giving them the authority to get it wrong in the process.

Safe to Fail

Shaping success in an ever-changing world means that teams must experiment with new ideas to adapt and better support their purpose. Experimentation with ideas only happens in an environment where people feel safe. Fear of making mistakes inhibits exploration and learning, and prevents people from speaking up when they see problems or asking for help when they need it. It is the role of the leader to create an environment of psychological safety so that people are comfortable to offer ideas, express concerns, show worry, ask for help, and learn from failure. People need a secure base.[39]

To build this environment, start weekly meetings by going around the room and having each person answer the question, "What did I learn last week that will help me be better next week?" The first person to answer this question should be the leader. Acknowledging that even the leader is learning and working on relentless ongoing improvement sends a message to everyone else that it is safe to do the same. The answer can be a process issue ("I found out that by requiring people to submit forms to me by 8:00 AM Monday, I was creating an unnecessary backlog") or a self-awareness issue ("I had no idea that when I come to meetings and I am deep in thought, some people think I am angry with them because I scowl when I think!"), or an admission of a knowledge gap ("I think I am making certain assumptions about our customers that I need to verify").

To create the mind-set of relentless ongoing improvement in project development, the After Action Review process used by the U.S. Army can be adapted for every stage of a team effort.[40] The process consists of the following questions, which can help a team find anomalies and shape opportunities for improvements.

1. What did we expect would happen?
2. What has actually happened?
3. Why is there a gap between what we expected and what occurred?
   a. What went better than expected and why?
   b. What went worse than expected and why?
4. What needs to change?

It is critical to compare expected results with actual results. This is where the learning begins. If there is a gap, was the problem one of assumptions, data, process, or technology? Based on the source of the anomaly, the team can learn what needs to improve, and generate ideas for change.

The Toyota method of analyzing gaps is to ask "Why?" five times, to get to root causes and make sure the real problem is addressed.[41] Let's use a hypothetical example of hospital operating rooms that are not being cleaned quickly enough for the next procedure to start on time.

A possible outcome of the five "whys" might sound like this:

Operating rooms are not being cleaned quickly enough between procedures.

Why? Because the facilities people are not arriving in time.

Why? Because they don't know when the last operation is ending.

Why? Because they work all over the building and don't have access to the information.

Why? Because we don't have a communication system to contact them.

Why? Because doctors and nurses have beepers but the facilities team does not.

Instead of yelling at the facilities team, or punishing them for being late, we now know that the real problem is a need to create a communication system so that they know when to arrive.

PRICE Strategy

To think about how to resolve gaps and solve a problem's root causes, a systematic approach to generate options is to use a PRICE strategy. PRICE is an acronym that invites ideas along four channels for change.[42]

P = Purpose: We first remind ourselves of the purpose or value we have aimed to create. Ideas for change will be evaluated based on their impact on improving our ability to deliver value.

R = Reduce: What should we do less of that will create better value? What would the customer love for us to do less of? Are we giving people more than they want? Are we doing so much we are overpromising and under-delivering?

I = Increase: What should we do more of? What would the customer love for us to do more of? What do people already like that we can leverage to create more value?

C = Create: What are we not doing at all that customers would love for us to add? What new activities or features can we create to better achieve our purpose?

E = Eliminate: What should we stop doing altogether? What is getting in the way of our ability to create value?

The team focuses their conversation on what they could potentially reduce, increase, create, or eliminate, to better serve the purpose in light of the gap discovered between what was expected and what actually happened. Ideas generated will need to be tested with the same attitude of experimentation—try them on a small scale, check outcomes against expectations, account for gaps, and continue to improve.

Experiment with ideas, and pause to check, learn, and refine. This is the model of relentless ongoing improvement.[43]

Desirable Failures

Linus Pauling, a two-time Nobel laureate, advised that "the best way to have a good idea is to have lots of ideas, and throw away the bad ones." We need, then, a strategy for generating lots of ideas, and a system for identifying the good ones.

Jim Lavoie is the chairman and former CEO of Rite-Solutions, an engineering and software company that started out in 2000 by building advanced systems for the Navy. Lavoie wanted to create a mechanism in his organization that could generate ideas continuously, with a process for surfacing the good ideas in a way that would not be demoralizing or threatening to those whose ideas were rejected. He experimented with a few methods that did not work—innovation summits (people had to wait with their ideas until these discrete events materialized), whiteboards all over the building (they tended to be empty most of the time), and an Innovation Room to foster creativity (people used the room to nap and snack more than to innovate).

None of these methods generated much innovation, so he kept thinking, and finally came up with a game based on the stock market. Anyone with an idea could launch it as a stock, and every employee was given $10,000 dollars of "opinion money" to invest in ideas they liked. In addition to purchasing stock, employees were encouraged to volunteer and collaborate to help develop and build the idea in which they had invested. The value of an idea would then be calculated based on the amount of peer-opinion money invested and people's willingness to work to develop it further. After launching the game in 2005, Lavoie was extremely impressed by its success at generating many ideas and quickly finding those that had the greatest value. Within a few years, employees had developed ideas that soon accounted for approximately 20 percent of the company's revenue.

The value of the game is that anybody and everybody is empowered to come up with ideas, and it provides a forum for quiet people to contribute in a safe and comfortable way, knowing that they can count on others to help the idea grow. Employees are also rewarded for their contributions. Ideas that lead to savings for the company result in a payoff to the investment team of 25 percent of the savings for a two-year period; ideas that lead to profits mean a reward of 25 percent of the profit over a two-year period to the team. Stocks that are not successful because people are not investing money or time soon see their price fall off the board, with no repercussions to the originator.

The architecture of the game makes it playful, participation is fun and rewarding, the ideas generated are varied and interesting, and the results are exactly what Lavoie wanted. What is very telling is that some of the proposals that became very successful were exactly the kind that Lavoie's executive team would have rejected had it been up to them to decide what constitutes a good idea. The desirable failures are the ideas that don't get traction, but that make it possible to float the ideas that enthusiastic people want to pursue further.[44]

The Virtual Laboratory

The Idea Stock Market mines the creative thinking inside organizations at all levels and across all functions. But it is limited to thinking from the inside. We also need to recognize that the "not invented here" attitude may quickly find us on the sidelines of a new game that people outside the organization are inventing. We turn to a health care company that found an effective way to discover and harness ideas being generated outside the organization.

A well-respected company that invents and distributes medical devices realized that their employees invent many successful products, but that at the same time there are more people who don't work for their company who might also be inventing potentially promising new products. They decided to create what they called the Virtual Laboratory. They would seek inventors who were at the beginning stages of an idea—perhaps graduate students in a university lab, or scientists tinkering in a garage—and give them seed money to develop their idea. But they wouldn't just invest in a handful of ideas—they would invest in hundreds of ideas. Because they were finding ideas at the beginning stages of design and experimentation, they could invest a little money in lots of ideas. The agreement between the company and the inventors stipulated that should the idea develop into a viable product, the device company would become the distributor.

The company to date has invested in hundreds of ideas. Only a handful of them have proved successful—but they tell us that the payoff from these successful products has more than covered the costs of all the other investments. It's a little bit like buying insurance into the future. We don't know what will work, so we embrace the uncertainty, try many things all at the same time, hedge our bets, and capture what unfolds.

InnoCentive

Another way to think about desirable failures is to acknowledge what you don't know and don't need to know in house, because somebody else can do it better and partnering with them can help you make your own weaknesses irrelevant. Amid the complexity and sheer number of issues facing organizations, you have to make strategic decisions about where you want to put your creative genius. For everything else, look for help.

This is where a company like InnoCentive, which we introduced in the last chapter, can add immense value. Companies such as Procter & Gamble, Boeing, Dow Chemicals, and DuPont recognize that they have a lot of smart people working for them, but that there are a lot of smart people who *don't* work for them, too. InnoCentive has registered thousands of globally diverse technical specialists across a wide spectrum of domains to serve as "problem solvers." These domain experts compete to solve the difficult challenges posed by "problem owner" companies who want to benefit from the brainpower outside their company. Each challenge has a deadline and an award, which to date can be as much as $100,000. With the rich variety of experiences these problem solvers bring to their thinking, many ideas can be generated around a single challenge, and through a filtering process the best idea is rewarded.[45]

Back to Linus Pauling

When generating lots of solutions around a single initiative or challenge, most of them fail to gain support—these are the desirable failures. Instead of endlessly debating over the ones that appear to be promising, create viable prototypes for multiple ideas, and experiment with them. Yet more ideas will fall into the failure bin. For those ideas still in the running, create more than one initial design for each, and compare and contrast them with quick, low-cost experiments. Here again, some of those initial designs won't work as well as others, but those desirable failures will spawn learning and better options. With a system for generating desirable failures in place, fewer unintentional failures occur when we finally create a product or service based on the winning solutions; and when those few unintentional mistakes do happen, we mine them for everything we can learn to continue the cycle of relentless ongoing improvement.

Unintentional Failures

Despite our best planning, experimenting, and testing of ideas, there will be times that the future will unfold and an idea we were sure would work is going to surprise us and fail. What we do with the failure will determine future opportunities.

Pause and Learn—Failures Can Create Opportunities

As a project evolves, look for unexpected outcomes and incongruities to find potential opportunities. A German chemist, Alfred Einhorn, synthesized Novocaine in 1905, and intended it to be used for major surgical operations. Surgeons were not impressed, preferring to use general anesthesia for surgical procedures; however, dentists found the new drug immensely appealing for their patients. Einhorn was appalled at this development, and spent the rest of his life traveling to dental schools to try to convince dentists not to use his drug because dentistry was not its intended use! He could not fathom or accept changing the path he had intended for his drug.[46]

Einhorn was unable to learn and profit from an unexpected outcome. In contrast, remember the story in Chapter 2 of the bicycle company that had developed a motorized bicycle to sell in India? They thought that with the difficult roads and lack of adequate transportation in India, people would jump at the chance to own a motorized bike. When farmers started to place orders for the motor alone, the company's first response was to refuse because they wanted to sell bicycles. Like Einhorn with his Novocaine, they had their intent and these orders were not aligned with that intent. Unlike Einhorn, the bicycle company acknowledged that the farmers had perceived a unique value in the product that they had never thought of. As a result, they changed their business and became one of the largest suppliers of mechanized water pumps in Southeast Asia.[47]

Many products we value today are the result of mistakes that were reframed into opportunity. Accidental, unplanned, unintentional consequences that could have been dismissed were instead leveraged.

Alexander Fleming never planned to invent penicillin. A Scottish bacteriologist, he was studying germs and doing an experiment with the deadly *Staphylococcus* bacterium in his lab. An assistant left a window open in the lab overnight, and when Fleming returned the next day he discovered that some mold had blown into the room and contaminated his experiment. With the bacteria now tainted, other scientists might have thrown the specimens away and started over. But Fleming was curious, and carefully inspected the bacteria under a microscope. He saw mold growing on the bacteria (darn, the original experiment was ruined), but was also shocked to see that around the mold there was a clear zone (Eureka!). Through the accidental contamination, Fleming gave the world penicillin, and in 1945 was awarded the Nobel Prize in Medicine.

Post-it Notes are another familiar product that was the result of an experiment gone wrong. Researchers at 3M were trying to invent a glue strong enough to hold together airplane parts. The resulting formula was so weak that the company didn't know what to do with it. The glue made objects stick to each other, but they could easily be separated. 3M shelved the formula. Six years later, in 1974, Arthur Fry, another 3M scientist, was frustrated because the little slips of paper he used to mark his hymnal when singing in his church choir kept falling out. He remembered the failed glue experiment, and thought he could use it for his page markers. 3M developed Post-it Notes from Fry's experiment, and tried to sell them in office supply stores in a few test markets. Sales were extremely poor and 3M considered once again shelving the glue. But Fry investigated, and realized that people were not buying the product because they had no idea what it was. He convinced 3M to give away samples in offices, and the rest is history. 3M began selling Post-it Notes in 1980 and they have become one of the most popular office products ever sold.

In the 1980s, Procter & Gamble tried to enter the bleach business. They had invented a color-safe bleach that could be used in cold water, and they were hoping it would be serious competition for the bleach leader, Clorox. They decided to test-market the product in Portland, Maine because it was so far from Clorox headquarters that maybe Clorox wouldn't notice. P&G created a major advertising campaign, established full retail distribution networks, and was ready to launch with samples and coupons. Just as the advertising campaign was about to start, Clorox gave a free gallon of Clorox bleach to every household in Portland, Maine, delivered straight to the front door. Nobody in Portland was going to need bleach for the next several months! Clorox had sent P&G a clear message. From this bleach failure, however, P&G took several lessons about how to defend brands, and they also created a new product by modifying the bleach formula and adding it to their laundry detergent, introduced as Tide with Bleach, which became a hugely successful product.[48]

Failures Can Solidify Relationships

How an organization responds to failure can be a defining moment in establishing credibility and deepening relationships with customers.

A remarkable construction company in California, founded by a legendary contractor named C.C. Myers, has time and again successfully done what many construction companies deem impossible. They complete projects in record time, adhering to the highest levels of safety, and at competitive cost. Their string of successes building roads, bridges, and highways spans several decades, going back to the founding of the company in 1977.

Despite a formidable number of achievements, what happened when things didn't go according to plan said more about this company than their successes. In 2003 it was building an elevated carpool lane in Orange County. Cracks were discovered in the concrete, ultimately putting the project two years behind schedule, and costing almost $4 million more than originally budgeted. Investigation showed that only part of the blame rested with the contractor. The Myers team could have walked away or tried to deflect blame elsewhere, but they accepted responsibility and absorbed the cost of the repairs. They worked with transit authorities to find solutions and remained committed to the project until it was completed. Their response to this failure enhanced their reputation and cemented their relationships in the industry.

The Myers team had years of success and interactions with transit authorities to build their trusted relationships before the carpool lane project ran into difficulty. What if your product or service fails before you have built up any relationship with your customer? Even here, your response can work to build trust rather than damage your reputation permanently. In 1989, the Lexus brand was launched, offering a new luxury vehicle to the American public with the tagline "The Relentless Pursuit of Perfection." Within three months 8,000 cars had been sold, only to have a faulty part discovered.[49] The irony was not lost on cynics and late-night comedians. Instead of trying to identify which of the cars were affected, Lexus turned it into a defining moment to demonstrate their commitment to customer care. They had dealers pick up all 8,000 cars, replace the part, and return the cars to their owners, washed and with a full tank of gas. Lexus leveraged this failure to show they were committed to the unfailing integrity of their relationship with the customer.

Successful Failing

Deliberate practice and desirable failure in a work or organizational context may look quite different from the type of deliberate practice and desirable difficulties recommended in sports or the arts. It may not require the refinement of fine motor skills, but the principles of the process remain relevant. Generating new ideas and filtering to find the good ideas, applying domain knowledge across multiple projects of increasing complexity, gathering information from others and integrating it appropriately, seeking evidence and feedback, creating a context that encourages learning from error, and responding with adaptive strategies are all part of the path to develop greater team and organizational success. As we quoted at the start of the chapter, Marion Blakey, chair of the FAA, succinctly said, "You can't leave a lasting footprint if you're always walking on tiptoe." So plant your feet at the starting line, take baby steps, and build the journey for your own enduring legacy. When you fall, get back up. Remember, you're not finished when you fail—you're only finished when you quit.

7

SHAPE YOUR FUTURE

Embrace Purpose, Engage People, Expand Possibilities

WE STARTED WITH A STORY, and we end with a story. The *Guinness Book of World Records* lists the Bible as the best-selling book of all time. One of the most universally familiar stories in the Bible is the account of Moses leading a nation out of bondage from Egypt. The story has endured the test of time because it is the story of an extraordinary journey to shape the future. Even though the story is thousands of years old, we can all relate it to our own odyssey because it is a story of purpose, hope, and resilience that are still part of the human experience.

The story begins with the Israelites enslaved in Egypt, yearning for freedom. Moses rose to prominence when he started the monumental task of leading them from slavery to liberty. If we look more closely at Moses as a leader,[1] we see he had qualities that each of us can nurture and develop to create our own extraordinary outcomes. Let's step back in time and into the story.

Moses was raised in the palace of Pharaoh and enjoyed wealth and power; in short, on the surface, he had it all. Yet he wrestled with deeper questions of morality and justice. Walking amongst the slaves he saw their plight and empathized with their suffering. In one instance, at great personal risk he stopped the brutal whipping of a slave, demonstrating that he put their welfare above his own, and earning their trust. In this act of justice we already see the first signs of Moses as a leader. He clearly believed in the dignity and value of each person. As we saw many times in this book, empathizing with the needs of others helps us to imagine new possibilities.

Moses took it upon himself soon thereafter to lead the oppressed people to freedom. This was not going to be easy for him. Moses knew he wasn't perfect; he had anger management problems, he had self-doubts, and he stuttered when he spoke. Understanding that he had to rise above his limitations and make his weaknesses irrelevant, from the beginning he engaged his brother Aaron to speak for him. He launched a campaign to convince Pharaoh to let the slaves leave Egypt, and at the same time began to prepare the people for the voyage ahead. Moses was hesitant and doubted he could fulfill the leadership position, especially in light of his speech impediment, but his strong sense of purpose propelled him to action.

Did Moses have the requisite skills to lead a nation? A leader does not necessarily have all the skills for the job. A leader is someone who sees a problem and does something about it, who stands up and says, "I will do what it takes to make this better." When Moses saw the suffering of the people, he saw a job that needed to be done, and chose to do it. You don't have to be perfect or certain of your success. You just have to choose. Anyone can daydream or wait for someone else to lead; extraordinary outcomes start by taking the first step.

It soon became clear that Pharaoh was not ready to agree to Moses's demands. After nine grueling rounds of negotiation trying to convince Pharaoh to release the slaves, Moses had failed to win him over. Winston Churchill once said that "success is moving from failure to failure with no loss of enthusiasm," and Moses certainly embodied this belief. He was not going to give up, and prepared to try to convince Pharaoh one more time. However, Moses also realized that he needed a Plan B, to be ready to act if he again failed to secure Pharaoh's consent. He devised a strategy for escape and sent instructions for the people to prepare resources so that they would be ready to leave the moment the opportunity presented itself. In the tenth attempt Pharaoh finally agreed to let the people go; since Moses had already prepared the people, he was able to quickly leverage the narrow window of opportunity and gave the signal to move.

Getting out of Egypt would not be an easy helicopter-on-the-rooftop rescue operation for the people; they would have to overcome their fears and make it happen. They would have to leave what they knew behind and venture into the unknown. Jack Welch has said that the role of a leader is to "define a vision and inspire your people to invent their way there." Moses began the undertaking with a clearly articulated and meaningful purpose: to take the people out of bondage and into the land where liberty and noble ideals could thrive. Leaving Egypt was only the beginning; it did not guarantee that they would arrive at their destination. The Israelites were longing to get out of slavery, but leaving something is not the same as working toward something. Moses had to create pictures of possibility to inspire people to overcome their fear of escape and invent their way to freedom.

The escape had all the makings of a Hollywood movie chase scene, including the obstacle of crossing the Red Sea, but the people prevailed. Once they reached the other side of the Red Sea they celebrated their victory, and in most tales this would be the end of the story. But in this epic, it is only the beginning. The people were about to enter a daunting world of uncertainty that would last for 40 years. Getting rid of Pharaoh would prove to be one of their easier challenges. Their new adversaries would be fears, doubts, and a mind-set of slavery they would have to overcome. In many ways, they would become their own worst enemy. The same is true for all of us; our biggest challenges can be our own beliefs and thoughts about what is possible, or as we called them earlier in the book, our elephant ropes.

After passing through the Red Sea, they traveled for three days without finding any water. When they finally found water, it was bitter and they complained to Moses about their thirst and hunger. Every time their survival was threatened, they denounced Moses and voiced regret that they had left Egypt. It's hard to let go of the familiar, even if it's not good for us. We saw the same issue in the story of Andy Grove, who had a hard time giving up the memory chip business because it was familiar, not because it was good for him or Intel. The people in the desert and Andy Grove both needed help to shift their mind-set. Grove took the counsel of Gordon Moore to transform his mind-set, and for the wanderers in the desert, Moses would have to guide them.

There would be many obstacles to overcome, and Moses had to develop a system for success. He would have to sustain the will of the people in the harsh and difficult desert conditions, and encourage them to continue the pursuit of purpose with unfailing commitment. It wasn't long before the people who had come out of slavery were in complete disarray and anarchy was rampant. One of Moses's first realizations was that this journey was going to be more difficult than he had imagined, and as a leader, he needed help. He had started his leadership as a micromanager, trying to solve every problem himself. It was as if an organizational chart had his name in every box. One day, his father-in-law, Jethro, was visiting and gave him some sage advice, essentially saying, "You are trying to do too much alone. You will wear yourself out and die. You need to create a system; appoint a small number of people to report to you, they will appoint others to report to them, and as teams working together, you will restore order." Jethro appears to be history's first recorded management consultant!

Moses showed himself to be a teachable leader. He listened to Jethro's advice and set up a system of distributed leadership. Each of the Twelve Tribes was given the autonomy to make decisions and solve problems. A council of 12 representatives, one from each tribe, convened with Moses on a regular basis to discuss issues before they became crises, and most likely to share stories of positive deviance so that other tribes could emulate and benefit.

Crossing the Sinai Desert should be a trip of days, perhaps weeks, but the Bible tells us that they wandered the desert for 40 years. Why did it take them so long? It was actually a purposeful procrastination. The people had escaped physical slavery but they were still slaves to their mind-set. To transform into a growth mind-set does not always come easily. We have to amplify the positive on the one hand, and at the same time acknowledge, learn, and correct by facing and over-coming the obstacles and difficulties that serve to shape us. For the people moving through the desert literally, and for each of us figura-tively, it happens one step at a time.

Moses had to adapt and deal with unexpected and difficult problems, both internally and from external enemies. Constantly seeking to improve his leadership, Moses eventually took some time off for reflection. Going up to Mount Sinai, he spent 40 days in solitary contemplation, seeking divine help, and asking aloud, "Why do I fail as I try different ways to inspire the people, and keep them focused on the ultimate goal, reaching the Promised Land?" In what could be described as the first executive retreat in recorded history, he finally understood that his role was to keep trying; to acknowledge failure, learn from each experience, and adapt to whatever would unfold. When he came back down from Mount Sinai and returned to the people, he brought with him a set of standards that resonate to this day. The Ten Commandments would become the enduring system for holding a people together.

To prepare for freedom, the people would have to develop the skills of responsibility, assertiveness, autonomy, and fortitude, and the adap-tive capacity to face the unknown. To guide them and help transform their mind-set, Moses did many of the things we discussed in this book:

- He kept them focused on the big picture and ultimate purpose; in fact, one day a week was set aside to revisit purpose and celebrate who they were and what they would become. Designating a day of rest and reflection was such a powerful strategy that it became a universal standard, and to this day it is found in every nation and culture in the world.
- He communicated many uplifting and inspiring messages of hope throughout the journey.
- He delivered a set of 10 standards, and added a codified set of laws to define how they would live up to these standards.
- He developed systems of self-rule, governance, and justice, to create the environment for growth.
- He created holidays to celebrate victories large and small. On the anniversary of the second year, the people began to celebrate their victory of leaving Egypt, a celebration Jews continue to mark every year with a Passover dinner and retelling of the Exodus story.

As the years wore on, Moses realized that he would have to partner with the future. Consequently, he chose to mentor Joshua and a group of young people from the next generation, who would outlive him and become his successors to realize the purpose and fulfill the ultimate goal. In this act, he practiced the principle of bringing the future to the present.

In 1776, the Founding Fathers of the United States turned to the Exodus story when they sought an emblem to represent what they were trying to forge. On the day the Declaration of Independence was signed, Benjamin Franklin, Thomas Jefferson, and John Adams were given the task of creating the Great Seal of the United States. Benjamin Franklin proposed to show Moses standing on the shore, extending his hand over the sea. In building a new nation, the Founders drew a parallel between the Israelites' deliverance from Egypt and their own deliverance from English rule. The final emblem has symbols from the story of Exodus and depicts an unfinished pyramid with 13 layers of stones (symbolizing the 13 states) but includes empty room at the top for more layers. Did they know more states would be added? Perhaps they recognized the value of an adaptive plan, incorporating slack to expand possibilities for whatever the future might bring.

The story of Moses embodies many of the principles we have discussed in this book. We can use the story metaphorically to map our own journey as we cross our personal seas and navigate across our own deserts in pursuit of purpose. We designed the following questions to trigger your thinking and help you generate ideas to shape your future.

1. Who or what is your Pharaoh, telling you that you can't move forward?
2. What do you want to stop doing or move away from?
3. What is your purpose that you want to move toward?
4. What will it take to ignite you to take action?
5. What are the standards you expect of yourself?
6. How will you breathe life into the standards?
7. Are you leveraging windows of opportunity?
8. How are you bringing the future to the present to eliminate and reduce uncertainty where possible?
9. What kind of adaptive plan do you have to embrace the unknown and thrive?
10. Who is on the journey with you, and who currently is not, but should be?
11. How are you building resilience together with your team?
12. What are you doing to develop your skill set?
13. What if you fail along the way? What is your failure protocol?

From Moses to Coach K and the many other stories we have shared with you, we have demonstrated that to create extraordinary outcomes in a world of uncertainty is a lifelong process of learning and transformation. We hope that you will find personally relevant ways to adopt the principles in this book to embrace purpose, engage people, and expand possibilities to shape your future.

Acknowledgments

BETWEEN THE TWO OF US, we have been at UCLA for over 100 years! We started as undergraduates, both earned our PhD (Moshe in Engineering and Applied Science, Iris in Cognitive Psychology), and now, we continue at UCLA as professors. We are deeply indebted to Victor Tabbush, professor emeritus and former associate dean, who built a bridge for us from Engineering and Psychology to the Anderson School, bringing us over to teach in MBA and Executive Programs. Years ago, he had the insight that the world is shrinking and that extraordinary outcomes come from multidisciplinary collaborations. Kelly Bean, associate dean of Executive Education, has continued to make it a joy for us to work at Anderson. Victor, and now Kelly, have helped us offer a unique program for executives, an annual five-day course entitled "Creativity and Innovation in the Organization." More than 1,000 executives have participated in the program, and to all of them we owe thanks for the sparks they ignited and stories they shared, which have helped us refine our thinking and develop the ideas in this book.

There are two people at UCLA who have been a source of inspiration and a font of knowledge, without whom this book would not have been possible. Elizabeth and Bob Bjork are mentors, colleagues, and friends. Much of their research shaped our thinking for Chapter 6. We look forward to many more years of learning from you.

We also have been working with organizations for many years, with people who want to shape extraordinary outcomes. Special thanks to the many individuals and teams who have collaborated with us and helped to bring our ideas to life. We have thanked you personally over the years and take this opportunity to thank you again.

Authors are always indebted to family for their support in making writing possible and in our case, it takes on greater meaning. We are a father-daughter team and the experience of writing this book together has been nothing short of, well, extraordinary! The family connection did not stop with us; Zaffa Rubinstein (mom and wife) willingly read the chapters and encouraged us to keep writing; Ayelet Firstenberg (daughter and granddaughter) spent untold hours helping us revise the manuscript many times, and every comment she made improved our writing; and Shmulik Firstenberg (husband and son-in-law) helped find just the right word when it was missing and knew exactly when to bring another cup of hot tea to fuel the creative juices. And of course, what makes our lives extraordinary are all the family who celebrate life with us; Zaffa, Shmulik, Noga and Oren, Ayelet, Gali, Dorit and Aaron, Marco, Evan, and Liza.

When we thought the manuscript was finally ready, our wonderful team at John Wiley & Sons, Inc., helped us see that the end is never actually the end. Special thanks to our editor, Richard Narramore, whose comments contributed greatly to the form and content of the book.

Notes

CHAPTER 1   SKILLS AND TALENT ARE NOT ENOUGH

1. Edmund L. Andrews, "Greenspan Concedes Error on Regulation," *New York Times*, October 23, 2008.

2. For more information on the journey of the U.S. Olympic men's basketball teams, see Mike Krzyzewski and Jamie K. Spatola, *The Gold Standard: Building a World-Class Team* (New York: Business Plus, 2010); David DuPree," U.S. Men's Basketball Falls Flat on World Stage," *USA Today*, August 15, 2004; Pete Thamel, "After Sitting in 2004, Ready to Stand and Deliver," *New York Times*, July 28, 2008; Kelly Whiteside, "Mike Krzyzewski for His Country: 'The Ultimate Honor,'" *USA Today*, July 20, 2012.

CHAPTER 2   CONNECT TO A COMPELLING PURPOSE

1. Viktor Frankl, *Man's Search for Meaning* (1959; repr., Boston: Beacon Press, 2006).

2. Warren Bennis and Patricia Ward Biederman, *Organizing Genius: The Secret of Creative Collaboration* (New York: Basic Books, 1998).

3. Mike Krzyzewski and Jamie K. Spatola, *The Gold Standard: Building a World-Class Team* (New York: Business Plus, 2010).

4. Ibid.

5. Barbara Waugh with Margot Silk Forrest, *The Soul in the Computer* (Maui, HI: Inner Ocean Publishing, 2001).

6. Gary Kelly, "Gary's Greeting: Happy Holidays! "*Spirit*, December 2013, 16, http://www.nxtbook.com/nxtbooks/pace/spirit_201312/index.php#/18.

7. Waugh, *The Soul in the Computer*.

8. Barbara Sher, *I Could Do Anything if I Only Knew What it Was* (New York: Dell, 1995).

9. Martin Seligman has authored three books through which we can follow the evolution of his thinking about happiness: *Authentic Happiness: Using the New Positive Psychology to Realize Your Potential for Lasting Fulfillment* (Free Press, 2002), *Learned Optimism: How to Change Your Mind and Your Life* (Vintage Books, 2006; originally published 1990), and *Flourish: A Visionary New Understanding of Happiness and Well-Being* (Free Press, 2011). For most of the history of psychology, researchers have investigated mental illness and psychological disorders. By contrast, Seligman's research looks at the other end of the spectrum: happiness and well-being.

10. Peter Drucker, *Innovation and Entrepreneurship* (1985; repr., New York: Harper Business, 2006).

CHAPTER 3   GALVANIZE YOUR TEAM

1. Mike Krzyzewski and Jamie K. Spatola, *The Gold Standard: Building a World-Class Team* (New York: Business Plus, 2010); Mike Krzyzewski and Jamie K. Spatola, *Beyond Basketball: Coach K's Keywords for Success* (New York: Business Plus, 2007); Jena McGregor, "Coach K's leadership ABCs," *The Washington Post*, November 11, 2011.

2. Jia-Rui Chong, "Nurses Find Hidden Cameras at Hospital," *Los Angeles Times*, November 18, 2004, http://articles.latimes.com/2004/nov/18/local/me-cameras18.

3. Our gratitude to Kelly Bean, associate dean of UCLA Executive Education, for sharing this insight with us. According to Kelly, people can only see your behavior; they can't see your intent, so act accordingly!

4. Personal communication with George Borst, 2010

5. Jana Matthews, "Spotlight on Growth: The Five Levels of Successful Delegation," The Jana Matthews Group, accessed April 4, 2014, http://janamatthewsgroup.com/images/resources/five-levels.pdf.

6. Michael Kosfeld et al., "Oxytocin Increases Trust in Humans," *Nature* 435, no. 2 (2005): 673–76, http://dept.wofford.edu/neuroscience/neuroseminar/pdffall2008/oxy-human.pdf.

7. Stephen Knack and Philip Keefer, "Does Social Capital Have an Economic Payoff? A Cross-country Comparison," *Quarterly Economic Journal* 112 (1997): 1251–88.

8. For a comprehensive review of the research on trust and economic progress, see Adolfo Morrone, Noemi Tontoranelli, and Giulia Ranuzzi, *How Good Is Trust? Measuring Trust and Its Role for the Progress of Societies*, OECD Statistics Working Papers 2009/03 (Paris: OECD Publishing 2009), http://dx.doi.org/10.1787/220633873086;

    For a review of research on the impact of trust in the workplace, see John Helliwell and Haifang Huang, *Well-being and Trust in the Workplace*, NBER Working Paper No. 14589 (Cambridge, MA: National Bureau of Economic Research, December 2008), http://www.nber.org/papers/w14589.pdf; John Helliwell and Haifang Huang, *How's the Job? Well-being and Social Capital in the Workplace*, NBER Working Paper 11759 (Cambridge, MA: National Bureau of Economic Research, November 2005), http://www.nber.org/papers/w11759.pdf.

9. For a review of research on the impact of trust on communities and nations, see Kenneth Arrow, "Gifts and Exchanges," *Philosophy and Public Affairs* 1, no. 4 (1972): 343–62; John Helliwell, *Understanding and Improving the Social Context of Well-being*, NBER Working Paper 18486 (Cambridge, MA: National Bureau of Economic Research, October 2012), http://faculty.arts.ubc.ca/jhelliwell/papers/w18486.pdf; Yann Algan and Pierre Cahuc, "Social Attitudes and Economic Development: An Epidemiological Approach," *VOX*, October 2, 2007, http://www.voxeu.org/article/trust-and-economic-development; Rafael Di Tella, Robert MacCulloch, and Andrew Oswald, "The Macroeconomics of Happiness," *Review of Economics and Statistics* 85, no. 4 (2003): 809–27; Francis Fukuyama, *Social Capital and Civil Society*, International Monetary Fund Working Paper WP/00/74, http://www.imf.org/external/pubs/ft/seminar/1999/reforms/fukuyama.htm; Francis Fukuyama "Social Capital and the Global Economy: A Redrawn Map of the World," *Foreign Affairs* 75, no. 4 (September/October 1995), http://www.foreignaffairs.com/articles/51402/francis-fukuyama/social-capital-and-the-global-economy-a-redrawn-map-of-the-world; Christiaan Grootaert and Thierry van Bastalear, eds., *The Role of Social Capital in Development: An Empirical Assessment* (Cambridge, UK: Cambridge University Press, 2008).

10. For a mnemonic strategy to learn names, see Harry Lorayne, *Remembering People: The Key to Success*, 2nd ed. (New York: Stein and Day, 1976).

11. Linda Stone coined the term *continuous partial attention*: http://lindastone.net/qa/continuous-partial-attention/.

12. The crossword analogy comes from David Shipley and Will Schwalbe in *Send* (New York: Vintage Books, 2010).

13. Jonathan Spira and Cody Burke, *Intel's War on Information Overload: A Case Study* (New York: Basex, Inc., August 2009), http://iorgforum.org/wp-content/uploads/2011/06/IntelWarIO.BasexReport1.pdf.

14. G.E. Cooper, M.D. White, and J.K. Lauber, eds., Resource Management on the Flight deck: Proceedings of a NASA/Industry Workshop (NASA CP-2120) (Moffett Field, CA: NASA-Ames Research Center, 1980).

15. American Psychological Association, "Making Air Travel Safer through Crew Resource Management," February 2014, https://www.apa.org/research/action/crew.aspx; David Bates and Atul Gawande "Error in Medicine: What Have We Learned?" *Annals of Internal Medicine* 132, no. 9 (May 2, 2000): 763–67, http://www.atulgawande.com/documents/Errorin-medicineWhathavewelearned.pdf; David P. Baker, Rachel Day, and Eduardo Salas, "Teamwork as an Essential Component of High-Reliability Organizations," *Health Services Research* 41, no. 4, pt. 2 (2006): 1576–98, http://www.ncbi.nlm.nih.gov/pmc/articles/PMC1955345/; S. S. Awad et al., "Bridging the Communication Gap in the Operating Room with Medical Team Training," *American Journal of Surgery* 190, no. 5 (2005): 770–74, http://www.ncbi.nlm.nih.gov/pubmed/16226956.

16. For an enlightening discussion of system design that takes into account human unreliability, see Donald Norman, *The Design of Everyday Things: Revised and Expanded Edition* (New York: Basic Books, 2013).

17. The story about the meeting with Ahmed was originally published in one of our earlier books, Moshe Rubinstein and Iris Firstenberg, *Patterns of Problem Solving*, 2nd ed. (Upper Saddle River, NJ: Prentice Hall, 1994).

18. Naomi Eisenberger, "Broken Hearts and Broken Bones: A Neural Perspective on the Similarities between Social and Physical Pain," *Current Directions in Psychological Science* 21, no. 1 (2012): 42–47. See also Association for Psychological Science, "Broken Hearts Really Hurt," press release, February 21, 2012, http://www.psychologicalscience.org/index.php/news/releases/broken-hearts-really-hurt.html.

19. Matthew Leiberman, *Social* (New York: Crown, 2013).

20. Eric D. Wesselmann et al., "To Be Looked At as Though Air: Civil Attention Matters," *Psychological Science* 20, no. 10 (2012): 1–3.

21. Passage taken from a study conducted by John D. Bransford and Marcia K. Johnson, "Contextual Prerequisites for Understanding: Some Investigations of Comprehension and Recall," *Journal of Verbal Learning and Verbal Behavior* 11 (1972): 717–26.

22. Chip Heath and Dan Heath, *Made to Stick* (New York: Random House, 2007).

23. Giovanni Gavetti and Jan W. Rivkin, "How Strategists Really Think: Tapping the Power of Analogy," *Harvard Business Review*, April 2005.

24. George Loewenstein, "The Psychology of Curiosity: A Review and Reinterpretation," *Psychological Bulletin* 116, no. 1 (1994): 75–98.

25. This method is recommended by Yale professor Edward Tufte, a pioneer in data visualization research. His books are widely regarded and include *The Cognitive Style of PowerPoint* (Graphics Press, 2006), *The Visual Display of Quantitative Information* (Graphics Press, 2001), and *Envisioning Information* (Graphics Press, 1990).

26. Edward Tufte presented to the Columbia Accident Investigation Board. His presentation, "PowerPoint Does Rocket Science—and Better Techniques for Technical Reports," can be found at http://www.edwardtufte.com/bboard/q-and-a-fetch-msg?msg_id=0001yB.Tufte's findings also appear in chapter 7 of the *Report of Columbia Accident Investigation Board*, "The Accident's Organizational Causes" (Washington, DC: U.S. Government Printing Office, August 2003), p. 15, http://anon.nasa-global.speedera.net/anon.nasa-global/CAIB/CAIB_lowres_chapter7.pdf.

27. We first presented the concept of YO in Moshe Rubinstein and Iris Firstenberg, *The Minding Organization* (Hoboken, NJ: John Wiley & Sons, 1999).

28. Jody Hoffer Gittell, *The Southwest Airlines Way* (New York: McGraw-Hill, 2005). A summary can be read at http://www.theclci.com/resources/The-SouthwestAirlinesWay.pdf.

CHAPTER 4   AMPLIFY THE POSITIVE

1. Gallup, *State of the American Workplace: Employee Engagement Insights for U.S. Business Leaders* (Washington, DC: Gallup, 2013), http://www.gallup.com/file/strategicconsulting/163007/State%20of%20the%20American%20Workplace%20Report%202013.pdf.

2. Joseph A. Michelli, *The New Gold Standard* (New York: McGraw Hill, 2008).

3. Personal communication with Aruna Raghavan, e-mail, December 10, 2012.

4. Michelli, *The New Gold Standard*.

5. Bonnie Rochman, "Executive Parenting," *Time*, March 25, 2013.

6. Mike Krzyzewski and Jamie K. Spatola, *The Gold Standard: Building a World-Class Team* (New York: Business Plus, 2010).

7. John Bargh, Mark Chen, and Lara Burrows, "Automaticity of Social Behavior: Direct Effects of Trait Construct and Stereotype Activation on Action," *Journal of Personality and Social Psychology* 71, no. 2 (1996): 230–44.

8. Aaron C. Kay et al., "Material Priming: The Influence of Mundane Physical Objects on Situational Construal and Competitive Behavioral Choice," *Organizational Behavior and Human Decision Processes* 95, no. 1 (2004): 83–96.

9. Margaret Shih, Todd L. Pittinsky, and Nalini Ambady, "Stereotype Susceptibility: Identity Salience and Shifts in Quantitative Performance," *Psychological Science* 10, no. 1 (1999): 80–83.

10. Jonah Berger, Marc Meredith, and S. Christian Wheeler, "Can Where People Vote Influence How They Vote? The Influence of Polling Location Type on Voting Behavior," Stanford Graduate School of Business Research Paper No. 1926, February 2006, https://gsbapps.stanford.edu/researchpapers/library/RP1926.pdf.

11. Norman Doidge, *The Brain That Changes Itself* (New York: Penguin, 2007).

12. Charles Darwin, *The Expression of the Emotions in Man and Animals* (London: John Murray, 1872).

13. William James published *The Principles of Psychology*, a comprehensive introduction to the field, in 1890. For a much shorter introduction to his views on emotion, read the 1884 article, "What Is an Emotion?" It can be accessed online at http://psychclassics.yorku.ca/James/emotion.htm.

14. For details of these Botox studies, see Eric Finzi, *The Face of Emotion: How Botox Affects our Moods and Relationships* (New York: Palgrave Macmillan, 2013). Also, see David A. Havas et al., "Cosmetic Use of Botulinum Toxin-A Affects Processing of Emotional Language," *Psychological Science* 21, no. 7 (2010): 895–900.

15. Michael Treadway et al., "Dopaminergic Mechanisms of Individual Differences in Human Effort-Based Decision Making," *The Journal of Neuroscience* 32, no. 18 (2012): 6170–6176.

16. F. Gregory Ashby, Alice Isen, and U. Turken, "A Neuropsychological Theory of Positive Affect and Its Influence on Cognition," *Psychological Review* 106, no. 3 (1999): 529–50. For more on the effects of smiling, see Marianne LaFrance, *Why Smile: The Science Behind Facial Expressions* (New York: W.W. Norton, 2013); Carl Charnetski and Francis X. Brennan, *Feeling Good Is Good for You: How Pleasure Can Boost Your Immune System and Lengthen Your Life* (Emmaus, PA: Rodale Books); Daniel N. McIntosh, "Facial Feedback Hypotheses: Evidence, Implications, and Directions," *Motivation and Emotion* 20, no. 2 (1996): 121–47; Chris L. Kleinke, Thomas R. Peterson, and Thomas R. Rutledge, "Effects of Self-generated Facial Expressions on Mood," *Journal of Personality and Social Psychology* 74, no. 1 (1998): 272–79; Pamela Adelmann and Richard Zajonc, "Facial Efference and the Experience of Emotion," *Annual Review of Psychology* 40 (1989): 249–80; and Fritz Strack, Leonard L. Martin,

and Sabine Stepper, "Inhibiting and Facilitating Conditions of the Human Smile: A Nonobtrusive Test of the Facial Feedback Hypothesis," *Journal of Personality and Social Psychology* 54 (1988): 768–77.

17. Dana R. Carney, Amy J. Cuddy, and Andy J. Yap, "Power Posing: Brief Nonverbal Displays Affect Neuroendocrine Levels and Risk Tolerance," *Journal of the Association for Psychological Science* 21, no. 10 (2010): 1363–68. See also Amy Cuddy's TED Talk, "Your Body Language Shapes Who You Are," at http://www.ted.com/talks/amy_cuddy_your_body_language_shapes_who_you_are.html.

18. Nicole M. Hill and Walter Schneider, "Brain Changes in the Development of Expertise: Neuroanatomical and Neurophysiological Evidence about Skill-Based Adaptations," in *The Cambridge Handbook of Expertise and Expert Performance*, eds. K. Anders Ericsson et al. (New York: Cambridge University Press, 2006), 653–82.

19. Marian Zeitlin, Hossein Ghassemi, and Mohamed Mansour, *Positive Deviance in Child Nutrition (with Emphasis on Psychosocial and Behavioural Aspects and Implications for Development)*, United Nations University, 1990, http://www.positivedeviance.org/pdf/publication%20nutrition/1990%20zeitlin%20posdev.pdf.

20. Richard Pascale, Jerry Sternin, and Monique Sternin, *The Power of Positive Deviance: How Unlikely Innovators Solve the World's Toughest Problems* (Boston: Harvard Business Review Press, 2010).

21. Much has been written about the contribution of Ignaz Semmelweis. See, for example, Arvind Singhal et al., "Spanning Silos and Spurring Conversations: Positive Deviance for Reducing Infection Levels in Hospitals," *Performance* 2, no. 3 (2009): 78–83, http://www.positivedeviance.org/pdf/Singhal-McCandless-Buscell-Lindberg-MRSA-Performance%202009-Article-EandY-2.pdf; K. Codell Carter and Barbara Carter, *Childbed Fever: A Scientific Biography of Ignaz Semmelweis* (Piscataway, NJ: Transaction Publishers, 2005); Mary Bellis, "History of Antiseptics," accessed April 5, 2014, http://inventors.about.com/library/inventors/blantisceptics.htm.

22. Glen D. Braunstein, "Hospital Acquired Infections: A Costly, Lethal Scourge That We Must Labor to Wash Our Hands of," *Huffington Post*, April 23, 2012, http://www.huffingtonpost.com/glenn-d-braunstein-md/hospital-acquired-infections_b_1422371.html; Linda Kohn, Janet M. Corrigan, and Molla S. Donaldson, eds., *To Err Is Human: Building a Safer Health System* (Washington, DC: National Academies Press, 2000).

23. Hospitals have turned to positive deviance strategies to lower infection rates; see Singhal et al., "Spanning Silos"; Arvind Singhal and Prucia Buscell,

"From Invisible to Visible: Learning to See and Stop MRSA at Billings Clinic," Billings Clinic and Plexus Institute, in conjunction with the Positive Deviance Initiative, accessed April 5, 2014, http://www.positivedeviance.org/projects/Singhal-Billings%20Story-FINAL.pdf; Arvind Singhal and Karen Greiner, "*When the Task Is Accomplished, Can We Say We Did It Ourselves?*" *A Quest to Eliminate MRSA at the Veterans Health Administration's Hospitals in Pittsburgh*, Positive Deviance Initiative, Veterans Health Administration Pittsburgh Healthcare System, and the Plexus Institute, 2007, http://www.communicationforsocialchange.org/pdfs/Arvind-Greiner-Mazi12.pdf; Arvind Singhal and Karen Greiner, with Prucia Buscell (2007), "Do What You Can, with What You Have, Where You Are. A Quest to Eliminate MRSA at the VA Pittsburgh Healthcare System," Plexus Institute, *Deeper Learning* 1, no. 4, http://www.positivedeviance.org/projects/VAPHS_-Story_with_3_logos_final_2008.pdf.

24. "Starve problems and feed opportunities" is attributed to Peter Drucker, *The Effective Executive* (New York: Harper Business Essentials, 2006).

25. Katherine Mieszkowski, "Change—Barbara Waugh," *Fast Company*, November 30, 1998, http://www.fastcompany.com/36451/change-barbara-waugh.

26. Barbara Waugh with Margot Silk Forrest, *The Soul in the Computer* (Maui, HI: Inner Ocean Publishing, 2001).

27. Richard Tanner Pascale and Jerry Sternin, "Your Company's Secret Change Agents," *Harvard Business Review*, May, 2005.

28. Karl E. Weick, "Small Wins: Redefining the Scale of Social Problems," *American Psychologist* 39, no. 1 (1984): 40–49.

29. Malcolm Gladwell, *The Tipping Point* (New York: Back Bay Books, 2002); George L. Kelling and James Q. Wilson, "Broken Windows," *The Atlantic Monthly*, March, 1982.

30. See the work of the Bill & Melinda Gates Foundation at http://www.gatesfoundation.org/What-We-Do/Global-Development/Water-Sanitation-and-Hygiene/Partners.

31. Tony Hsieh, *Delivering Happiness* (New York: Business Plus, 2010).

32. David Gal and Blakeley McShane, "Can Small Victories Help Win the War? Evidence from Consumer Debt Management," *Journal of Marketing Research* 49, no. 4 (2012): 487–501.

33. For more on the miracle scale and how to apply it, see Michelle Weiner-Davis, *Change Your Life and Everyone In It* (New York: Simon & Shuster, 1996). Thanks to our friend Bob Maurer for the exercise example his book, *One Small Step Can Change Your Life: The Kaizen Way* (New York: Workman Publishing, 2004).

34. The field of Positive Psychology is flourishing. In addition to the books by Martin Seligman referenced earlier, we recommend the following: Shawn Achor, *The Happiness Advantage* (New York: Crown Business, 2010); Jonathan Haidt, *The Happiness Hypothesis* (New York: Basic Books, 2006); Dan Baker and Cameron Stauth, *What Happy People Know* (New York: St. Martin's Griffin, 2004); Tal Ben Shahar, *The Question of Happiness* (Bloomington, IN: Writers Club Press, 2002); Edward Deci with Richard Flaste, *Why We Do What We Do* (New York: Penguin Books, 1996).

35. Hsieh, *Delivering Happiness*.

36. Michael Abrashoff, *It's Your Ship* (New York: Business Plus, 2007).

37. Marcial Losada, "Work Teams and the Losada Line: New Results," *Positive Psychology News Daily*, December 9, 2008, http://positivepsychologynews. com/news/marcial-losada/200812091298.

   See also Barbara Fredrickson and Marcial Losada (2005), "Positive Affect and the Complex Dynamics of Human Flourishing," *American Psychologist* 60, no. 7 (2005): 678–86. The precise mathematical number for the Losada Ratio has been under debate, although there is support for the ratio in general. For discussion, see http://psycnet.apa.org/journals/amp/68/9/822; http:// retractionwatch.com/2013/09/19/fredrickson-losada-positivity-ratio-paper-partially-withdrawn/

38. Shelly L. Gable, Gian C. Gonzaga, and Amy Strachman, "Will You Be There for Me When Things Go Right?" *Journal of Personality and Social Psychology* 91, no. 5 (2006): 904–17.

39. Barbara Fredrickson, "The Role of Positive Emotions in Positive Psychology: The Broaden-and-Build Theory of Positive Emotions," *American Psychologist* 56, no. 3 (2001): 218–26; Barbara Fredrickson and Christine Branigan, "Positive Emotions Broaden the Scope of Attention and Thought-Action Repertoires," *Cognition and Emotion* 19, no. 3 (2005): 313–32.

40. For a review article, see Alice Isen, "The Influence of Positive Affect on Decision Making in Complex Situations: Theoretical Issues with Practical Implications," *Journal of Consumer Psychology* 11, no. 2 (2001): 75–85; Yaacov Trope and Eva M. Pomerantz, "Resolving Conflicts among Self-Evaluative Motives: Positive Experiences as a Resource for Overcoming Defensiveness," *Motivation and Emotion* 22 (1998): 53–72; Peter J. Carnevale and Alice Isen, "The Influence of Positive Affect and Visual Access on the Discovery of Integrative Solutions in Bilateral Negotiation," *Organizational Behavior and Human Decision Processes* 37 (1986): 1–13; Alice Isen, Kimberly Daubman, and Gary Nowicki, "Positive Affect Facilitates Creative

Problem Solving," *Journal of Personality and Social Psychology* 52 (1987): 1122–31.

41. Sigal Barsade and Donald Gibson, "Why Does Affect Matter in Organizations?" *Academy of Management Perspectives*, February 2007, 36–59; Carlos A. Estrada, Alice M. Isen, and Mark J. Young, "Positive Affect Facilitates Integration of Information and Decreases Anchoring in Reasoning among Physicians," *Organizational and Human Decision Processes* 72 (1997): 117–35; Carlos Estrada, Mark Young, and Alice Isen, "Positive Affect Improves Creative Problem Solving and Influences Reported Source of Practice Satisfaction in Physicians," *Motivation and Emotion* 18 (1994): 285–99; Barry M. Staw, Robert L. Sutton, and Lisa H. Pelled, "Employee Positive Emotion and Favorable Outcomes at the Workplace," *Organizational Science* 5, no. 1 (February 1994): 51–71; Carnevale and Isen, "Influence of Positive Affect."

42. Felicia Huppert, "Positive Emotions and Cognition: Developmental, Neuroscience, and Health Perspectives." In *Hearts and Minds: Affective Influences on Social Cognition and Behavior, Proceedings of the 8th Sydney Symposium* (New York: Psychology Press, 2008).

43. Ashby et al., "Neuropsychological Theory of Positive Affect"; Patricia S. Goldman-Rakic, "Cellular Basis of Working Memory," *Neuron* 14 (1995), 477–85.

44. Alessandro Tessitore et al., "Dopamine Modulates the Response of the Human Amygdala: A Study in Parkinson's Disease," *Journal of Neuroscience* 22, no. 20 (2002): 9099–9103; Thorsten Kienast et al., "Dopamine in Amygdala Gates Limbic Processing of Aversive Stimuli in Humans," *Nature Neuroscience* 11 (2008): 1381–2.

45. (ibid.) F. Gregory Ashby, Alice Isen, & And Turken (1999). "A neuropsychological theory of positive affect and its influence on cognition." *Psychological Review* 106 (3): 529–550. The anterior cingulate is involved in our ability to decide what information to pay attention to and what to ignore, and the striatum is key for cognitive flexibility, which is the ability to discern when the relative importance of factors in a decision is shifting. For more detail about the brain, see Ashby et al., "Neuropsychological Theory of Positive Affect."

CHAPTER 5   CONQUER UNCERTAINTY

1. One of the greatest advantages of our human mind is its ability to contemplate the future in the present. The shift from a Neanderthal brain focused entirely on the present, to a *Homo sapiens* brain that can conceive the future, made

possible the shift from raiding (grab someone's apples whenever you want them) to bartering (give me two of your apples and I'll give you two of my oranges). To enhance trade and exchange, our brains developed the abstract concept of money (give me two of your apples and, because you don't want my oranges, I'll give you money that you can use to get what you want at some future point). Money is effectively trust, inscribed as potential future value. If you want my apple, and you want to trade money for it, I have to understand and believe that accepting your money will enable me to get something that I will value at some future point in time. In effect, without a concept of the future, money would have no value.

Thus, the concepts of money and the future are linked; the concept of money cannot exist without a concept of the future.

2. The September 2011 edition of the *Harvard Business Review* spotlights issues of complexity in organizations. Articles include "Learning to Live with Complexity" by Gokce Sargut and Rita Gunter McGrath, "Smart Rules: Six Ways to Get People to Solve Problems without You" by Yves Morieux, and "Embracing Complexity" by Tim Sullivan.

For an interesting discussion of complexity in healthcare, see Sholom Glouberman and Brenda Zimmerman, *Complicated and Complex Systems: What Would Successful Reform of Medicare Look Like?* Discussion Paper No. 8, Commission on the Future of Health Care in Canada, 2002, http://publications.gc.ca/collections/Collection/CP32–79–8–2002E.pdf.

3. Niall Ferguson, *The Ascent of Money: A Financial History of the World* (New York: Penguin Books, 2009).

4. For a fun example of using story to improve memory, try the following exercise. Suppose you want to memorize the first 10 chemical elements of the periodic table. Listed in order, they are hydrogen, helium, lithium, beryllium, boron, carbon, nitrogen, oxygen, fluorine, and neon. Ed Cooke presented a story in the January 14, 2012, edition of *The Guardian*, which we have adapted below, to help you remember them. After reading the story, try to retrieve it from memory and you will see that you know the 10 elements in order. You may be surprised to see how well you remember the story even days from now.

> A nuclear bomb (hydrogen) is about to go off, but it is lifted up and whisked away by a (helium) balloon with a (lithium) battery. Down below, a lady named Beryl (beryllium) celebrates by cooking a boar (boron) over the engine of her car (carbon). Just then a knight (nitrogen) in shining armor, who is riding past on a big ox (oxygen),

sweeps Beryl up and takes her to a florist (fluorine) where he gets down on his knee (neon) and proposes marriage.

Adapted from Ed Cooke, "How Narratives Can Aid Memory," *The Guardian*, January 14, 2012, http://www.theguardian.com/lifeandstyle/2012/jan/15/story-lines-facts.

For the role of story in comprehension and memory, see Steven Pinker, *The Stuff of Thought* (New York: Penguin Books, 2008); Jerome Bruner, *Actual Minds, Possible Worlds* (Cambridge, MA: Harvard University Press, 1987); Roger Schank and Robert Abelson, "Knowledge and Memory: The Real Story," in *Knowledge and Memory: The Real Story*, ed. Robert S. Wyer Jr. (Mahwah, NJ: Lawrence Erlbaum Associates, 1995); and Richard Anderson, "Role of the Reader's Schema in Comprehension, Learning and Memory," in *Learning to Read in American Schools: Basal Readers and Content Texts*, eds. Richard Anderson, Jean Osborn, and Robert Tierney (Hillsdale, NJ: Lawrence Erlbaum Associates, 1984).

5. Antonio Damasio, *Descartes' Error: Emotion, Reason, and the Human Brain* (New York: Penguin Books, 2005).

6. To learn more about how to develop storytelling skills, we recommend Paul Smith, *Lead with a Story: A Guide to Crafting Business Narratives that Captivate, Convince, and Inspire* (New York: AMACOM, 2012); Lisa Cron, *Wired for Story: The Writer's Guide to Using Brain Science to Hook Readers from the Very First Sentence* (New York: Ten Speed Press, 2012); and Stephen Denning, *The Springboard: How Storytelling Ignites Action in Knowledge-Era Organizations* (Oxon, England: Routledge, 2011).

7. To see the e-publications, the GE Reports can be found at http://www.gereports.com, and Siemens's *Pictures of the Future* are at http://www.siemens.com/innovation/en/publications.

8. Jason Zweig, *Your Money and Your Brain* (New York: Simon & Schuster, 2008).

9. David Gergen, *Eyewitness to Power: The Essence of Leadership, Nixon to Clinton* (New York: Simon & Schuster, 2001).

10. Tara Siegel Bernard, "In Retreat, Bank of America Cancels Debit Card Fee," *New York Times*, November 1, 2011.

11. Stu Woo, "Under Fire, Netflix Rewinds DVD Plan," *Wall Street Journal*, October 11, 2011.

12. Meghan Casserly, "Dell's Revamped 'Della' Site for Women," *Forbes*, May 22, 2009, http://www.forbes.com/2009/05/22/dell-tech-marketing-forbes-woman-time-della.html.

13. We developed an early framework of deliberate and emergent chaos in our book, *The Minding Organization* (Hoboken, NJ: John Wiley & Sons, 1999).

14. Andy Grove, *Only the Paranoid Survive: How to Exploit the Crisis Points That Challenge Every Company* (New York: Crown Business, 1999).

15. For more on loss aversion and other cognitive biases that influence thinking, see Daniel Kahneman and Amos Tversky, "Choices, Values, and Frames," *American Psychologist* 39, no. 4 (1984): 341–50; Daniel Kahneman and Amos Tversky, "Prospect Theory: An Analysis of Decision under Risk," *Econometrica* 47, no. 2 (March 1979): 263–92; Daniel Kahneman, *Thinking, Fast and Slow* (New York: Farrar, Strauss and Giroux; 2011).

16. Roland G. Fryer Jr. et al., *Enhancing the Efficacy of Teacher Incentives through Loss Aversion: A Field Experiment*, NBER Working Paper No. 18237, JEL No. J24 (Cambridge, MA: National Bureau of Economic Research, July 2012), http://www.nber.org/papers/w18237.

17. For articles related to the Wakefield scandal and scare that ensued, see Kreesten Madsen et al., "A Population-Based Study of Measles, Mumps, and Rubella Vaccination and Autism," *New England Journal of Medicine* 347 (2002): 1477–82; Liz Szabo, "Full Vaccine Schedule Safe for Kids, No Link to Autism," *USA Today*, March 29, 2013, http://www.usatoday.com/story/news/nation/2013/03/29/vaccine-schedule-autism/2026617/; Gregory A. Poland, "MMR Vaccine and Autism: Vaccine Nihilism and Postmodern Science," *Mayo Clinic Proceedings* 86, no. 9 (September 2011): 869–71, http://www.mayoclinicproceedings.org/article/S0025–6196(11)65218-X/fulltext; Alexandra Sifferlin, "Parents Not Vaccinating Kids Contributing to Whooping Cough Outbreaks," *Time Health & Family*, September 30, 2013, http://healthland.time.com/2013/09/30/parents-not-vaccinating-kids-contributed-to-whooping-cough-outbreaks/; Kate Rope, "The End of the Autism/Vaccine Debate?" *CNN Health*, September 10, 2010, http://www.cnn.com/2010/HEALTH/09/07/p.autism.vaccine.debate/. The retracted *Lancet* article can be accessed at http://www.thelancet.com/journals/lancet/article/PIIS0140–6736(97)11096–0/abstract.

18. Our gratitude to Captain Gene Harris of the Monterey Park Police Department for sharing the term *build-in* with us.

19. Special thanks to Tom Hardy, VP of Finance at Amgen, for sharing this story with us.

20. Gibson quote in "High-Speed Internet Access: Broadband Blues." *The Economist*, June 21, 2001, www.economist.com/node/666610.

21. For the story of Pivot Planet, see https://www.pivotplanet.com/team#our-story.

22. We first told the story of Cemex in our book *The Minding Organization* (Hoboken, NJ: John Wiley & Sons, 1999).

23. Keith Peecock, A Risk Communication Success Story, NASA white paper, personal communication, November 13, 2012, http://www.google.com/url? sa=t&rct=j&q=&esrc=s&source=web&cd=7&ved=0CGQQFjAG&url= http%3A%2F%2Fntrs.nasa.gov%2Farchive%2Fnasa%2Fcasi.ntrs.nasa.gov% 2F20120002768.pdf&ei=-i5EU-78N4Tk2QWI2YCQ-BA&usg=AFQjCNGOHAH3IvHpW8u2sOnzK-6dVoDjXg&sig2=IuQZYs6PhuAHdcJXlJAZjw].

24. Eliot Van Buskirk, "Winning Teams Join to Qualify for $1 Million Netflix Prize," *Wired*, June 26, 2009, http://www.wired.com/business/2009/06/winning-teams-join-to-qualify-for-1-million-netflix-prize/.

25. Cornelia Dean, "If You Have a Problem, Ask Everyone," *New York Times*, July 22, 2008, http://www.nytimes.com/2008/07/22/science/22inno.html? pagewanted=all&_r=0.

26. David Smith, "Proof! Just Six Degrees of Separation Between Us," *The Observer*, August 2, 2008, http://www.theguardian.com/technology/2008/ aug/03/internet.email.

27. For details on the strategy, see http://www.thegreatschlep.com/schlep-labs.

28. Michael Scherer, "Friended: How the Obama Campaign Connected with Young Voters," *Time*, December 3, 2012, http://swampland.time.com/2012/ 11/20/friended-how-the-obama-campaign-connected-with-young-voters/.

29. Karl Greenberg, "Acura, W Hotels to Promote MDX Crossover," *Marketing Daily*, March 16, 2011, http://www.mediapost.com/publications/article/ 146846/. See also We Drive U, "Case Study: Experiential Marketing," accessed April 8, 2014, http://www.wedriveu.com/index.php/case-study-experiential-marketing.

30. Exerting self-control requires glucose as an energy source. A single act of self-control causes glucose levels to drop below optimal levels, impairing subsequent attempts at self-control. See Matthew T. Gailliot et al., "Self-control Relies on Glucose as a Limited Energy Source: Willpower Is More Than a Metaphor," *Journal of Personality and Social Psychology* 92, no. 2 (2007): 325–36.

31. Hal Ersner-Hershfield, G. Elliott Wimmer, and Brian Knutson, "Saving for the Future Self: Neural Measures of Future Self Continuity Predict Temporal Discounting," *Social Cognitive and Affective Neuroscience* 4, no. 1 (2009): 85–92.

32. Shlomo Benartzi, *Behavioral Finance in Action*, Allianz Center for Behavioral Finance white paper, June 1, 2012, http://befi.allianzgi.com/en/Topics/ Documents/behavioral-finance-in-action-white-paper.pdf; Shlomo Benartzi,

Save More Tomorrow: Practical Behavioral Finance Solutions to Improve 401(k) Plans (New York: Portfolio Hardcover, 2012); Richard Thaler and Shlomo Benartzi, "Save More Tomorrow™: Using Behavioral Economics to Increase Employee Saving," *Journal of Political Economy* 112, no. 1 (2004): 164–87.

33. Russia Financial Literacy and Education Trust Fund, *Improving Financial Education Effectiveness through Behavioural Economics: OECD Key Findings and Way Forward*, June 2013, http://www.oecd.org/daf/fin/financial-education/TrustFund2013_OECDImproving_Fin_Ed_effectiveness_through_Behavioural_Economics.pdf.

34. Hal E. Hershfield et al., "Increasing Saving Behavior through Age-Progressed Renderings of the Future Self," *Journal of Marketing Research* 48 (2011): 23–27, http://people.stern.nyu.edu/hhershfi/resources/Research/JMR-D-ce.pdf.

35. "Fashion Forward," *The Economist*, March 22, 2012, http://www.economist.com/node/21551063; "The Future of Fast Fashion," *The Economist*, June 16, 2005, http://www.economist.com/node/4086117; "Floating on Air: Spain's Zara," *The Economist*, May 17, 2001, http://www.economist.com/node/627426.

36. For information about the history of time zones in the United States, see "Nov 18, 1883: Railroads Create the First Time Zones," History.com, accessed April 8, 2014, http://www.history.com/this-day-in-history/railroads-create-the-first-time-zones; "Today in History: November 18—Time!" Library of Congress, last modified November 4, 2010, http://memory.loc.gov/ammem/today/nov18.html.

37. For additional details on the Cemex story, see our book *The Minding Organization* (Hoboken, NJ: John Wiley & Sons, 1999); Rosabeth Moss Kanter, *SuperCorp: How Vanguard Companies Create Innovation, Profits, Growth, and Social Good* (New York: Crown Business, 2009); Rosabeth Moss Kanter, "Transforming Giants," Harvard Business Review, January 2008, http://hbr.org/2008/01/transforming-giants/ar/1; Thomas Petzinger Jr., "In Search of the New World (of Work)," *Fast Company*, March 31, 1999, http://www.fastcompany.com/36625/search-new-world-work.

38. Kevin Kelleher, "*The Wired 40*," *Wired*, July 2003.

39. Lisa Earle McLeod, "How P&G, Southwest, and Google Learned to Sell with Noble Purpose," *Fast Company*, November 29, 2012, http://www.fastcompany.com/3003452/how-pg-southwest-and-google-learned-sell-noble-purpose.

40. Daniel Kahneman and Amos Tversky coined the term *cognitive biases* in 1974, and demonstrated their impact on decision making. Their research earned

Kahneman the Nobel Prize in Economics in 2002 (Tversky unfortunately had died, and the Nobel is not awarded posthumously). Several enlightening books documenting cognitive biases include Daniel Kahneman, *Thinking, Fast and Slow*; Sydney Finkelstein, Jo Whitehead, and Andrew Campbell, *Think Again: Why Good Leaders Make Bad Decisions and How to Keep It from Happening to You* (Boston: Harvard Business Review Press, 2009); Dan Ariely, *Predictably Irrational* (New York: HarperCollins, 2008); Richard H. Thaler and Cass R. Sunstein, *Nudge: Improving Decisions about Health, Wealth, and Happiness* (New Haven, CT: Yale University Press, 2008); Jerome Groopman, *How Doctors Think* (New York: Houghton Mifflin, 2007); Carol Tavris and Elliot Aronson, *Mistakes Were Made (But Not By Me): Why We Justify Foolish Beliefs, Bad Decisions, and Hurtful Acts* (Boston: Harcourt, 2007).

41. Groopman, *How Doctors Think*.

42. Daniel Kahneman, Dan Lovallo, and Olivier Sibony, "Before You Make That Big Decision," *Harvard Business Review*, June 2011, http://hbr.org/2011/06/the-big-idea-before-you-make-that-big-decision/ar/1.

43. Andis Robeznieks, "Building a Nimble Hospital," *Modern Healthcare*, February 16, 2013, http://www.modernhealthcare.com/article/20130216/MAGAZINE/302169954.

44. Emily Melina and Kara Shuler, "What Darwin Can Teach Government," Deloitte University Press Gov Lab report, July 31, 2013, http://dupress.com/articles/what-darwin-can-teach-government-harnessing-positive-deviants-to-help-solve-vexing-problems-within-your-organization/.

45. Lars Thuesen, "The Secret Behaviour of Local Heroes in the Danish Prison Service," in Kriminal Forsorgen and Woodward Lewis Group Report, *Radical Problem Solving Approach Delivers Results for Community and Organisational Issues—by Revealing What Is Already Working*, accessed December 31, 2013, http://www.cambridgeshire.gov.uk/NR/rdonlyres/92567DFF-8BFA-4037-9B3A-29712E056AE2/0/PositiveDeviancecasestudies.pdf.

46. Sheena Iyengar, *The Art of Choosing* (New York: Twelve, 2010); Barry Schwarz, *The Paradox of Choice* (New York: Ecco, 2003).

47. Thaler and Sunstein, *Nudge*; Olivia Mellan and Sherry Christie, "Too Many Choices: How to Help Clients Decide," *Investment Advisor*, December, 2013, http://www.thinkadvisor.com/2013/11/25/too-many-choices-how-to-help-clients-decide.

48. David Freedman, "Corps Values," *Inc.*, April 1998, http://www.inc.com/magazine/19980401/906.html.

49. Eric Bonabeau and Christopher Meyer, "Swarm Intelligence: A Whole New Way to Think about Business," *Harvard Business Review*, May 2001, http://

hbr.org/2001/05/swarm-intelligence-a-whole-new-way-to-think-about-business/ar/1.

50. Nobuo Sato and Mayuka Yamazaki, "How Generation Next Is Rebuilding Japan," *Harvard Business Review Blog Network*, May 17, 2011, http://blogs.hbr.org/2011/05/how-generation-next-is-rebuild/.

51. Special thanks to our friend, Noshir Kathok, for introducing us to the *dabbawala* phenomenon.

   For more information, see Stefan Thomke, "Mumbai's Models of Service Excellence," *Harvard Business Review*, November 2012, http://hbr.org/2012/11/mumbais-models-of-service-excellence/ar/1; Karl Moore, "The Best Way to Innovation? An Important Lesson from India," *Forbes*, May 24, 2011, http://www.forbes.com/sites/karlmoore/2011/05/24/the-best-way-to-innovation-an-important-lesson-from-india/.

CHAPTER 6 ACKNOWLEDGE, LEARN, CORRECT

1. Steven Spielberg was interviewed on the CBS show *Sunday Morning* on July 4, 2010. Transcript available online at http://www.cbsnews.com/news/lucas-and-spielberg-on-norman-rockwell/.

2. Dan Baker, *What Happy People Know* (New York: St. Martin's Griffin, 2004).

3. Bob Willis, "The More Americans Make, the Higher 'Rich' Becomes, Gallup Says," *Bloomberg BusinessWeek*, December 19, 2011, http://www.businessweek.com/news/2011-12-19/the-more-americans-make-the-higher-rich-becomes-gallup-says.html.

4. Sheryl Sandberg, *Lean In* (New York: Knopf, 2013).

5. Patrick Enright, "Even Stars Get Stage Fright," NBCnews.com, September 12 2007, http://www.nbcnews.com/id/20727420/ns/health-mental_health/t/even-stars-get-stage-fright/.

6. For more information on Imposter Syndrome, see the January 28, 2014, issue of *The Huffington Post*, which was dedicated to Imposter Syndrome, at http://www.huffingtonpost.com/news/imposter-syndrome.

7. Martin Seligman (2006). *Learned Optimism: How to Change Your Mind and Your Life* (New York: Vintage Books, 2006).

8. Carol Dweck, *Mindset: The New Psychology of Success* (New York: Ballantine, 2007).

9. Bonnie St. John, *Live Your Joy* (New York: FaithWords, 2009).

10. The heading is a quote from George Bernard Shaw.

11. Dweck, *Mindset*.

12. Carol Dweck, "The Mindset of a Champion," *Campus Perspectives* (blog), accessed April 9, 2014, http://champions.stanford.edu/perspectives/the-mindset-of-a-champion/.

13. Peter A. Heslin and Don VandeWalle, "Managers' Implicit Assumptions about Personnel," *Current Directions in Psychological Science* 17, no. 3 (2008): 219–23.

14. Marian Diamond, *Enriching Heredity: The Impact of the Environment on the Anatomy of the Brain* (New York: Free Press, 1988); Marian Diamond and Janet Hopson, *Magic Trees of the Mind: How to Nurture Your Child's Intelligence, Creativity, and Healthy Emotions from Birth Through Adolescence* (New York: Plume, 1999).

15. For the study on managers, see Peter Heslin, Don VandeWalle, and Gary Latham (2006). "Keen to Help? Managers' Implicit Person Theories and Their Subsequent Employee Coaching," *Personnel Psychology* 59 (2006): 871–902, http://dvandewalle.cox.smu.edu/Keen%20to%20help_Managers'%20IPTs%20and%20their%20subsequent%20employee%20coaching.pdf.
    For the study on athletes, see Dweck, "The Mindset of a Champion." For more applications, see Janet Rae-Dupree, "If You're Open to Growth, You Tend to Grow," *New York Times*, July 6, 2008, http://www.nytimes.com/2008/07/06/business/06unbox.html?_r=0.

16. Albert Ellis and Arthur Lange, *How to Keep People from Pushing Your Buttons* (New York: Kensington Publishing Corp., 1994); Albert Ellis and Robert Harper, *A Guide to Rational Living* (Chatsworth, CA: Wilshire Book Company, 1975).

17. Maladaptive thinking leads to distortions in our perception and interpretation of events. For examples of these distortions, see John Grohol, "15 Common Cognitive Distortions," *Psych Central*, July 25, 2013, http://psychcentral.com/lib/15-common-cognitive-distortions/0002153.

18. Matthew Lieberman et al., "Putting Feelings into Words: Affect Labeling Disrupts Amygdala Activity in Response to Affective Stimuli," *Psychological Science* 18, no. 5 (May 2007): 421–28, http://www.scn.ucla.edu/pdf/AL(2007).pdf.

19. Robert Weisberg, "Modes of Expertise in Creative Thinking: Evidence from Case Studies," in *The Cambridge Handbook of Expertise and Expert Performance*, eds. K. Anders Ericsson et al. (New York: Cambridge University Press, 2006), 761–87; John Hayes, "Cognitive Process in Creativity," *Handbook of Creativity*, eds. John A. Glover, Royce R. Ronning, and Cecil R. Reynolds (New York: Plenum, 1989), 135–45.

20. Bruce Weber, "Bobby Fischer, Troubled Genius of Chess, Dies at 64," *New York Times*, January 19, 2008, http://www.nytimes.com/2008/01/19/crosswords/chess/19fischer.html?pagewanted=3&_r=0.

21. Weisberg, "Modes of Expertise in Creative Thinking."

22. Malcolm Gladwell, *Outliers* (New York: Bay Back Books, 2011).

23. Ericsson et al., *The Cambridge Handbook of Expertise and Expert Performance*.

24. K. Anders Ericsson, ed., *The Road to Excellence: The Acquisition of Expert Performance in the Arts and Sciences, Sports, and Games* (Mahwah, NJ: Lawrence Erlbaum Associates, 1996); K. Anders Ericsson, Ralf Krampe, and Clemens Tesch-Romer, "The Role of Deliberate Practice in the Acquisition of Expert Performance," *Psychological Review* 100, no. 3 (1993): 363–406; Robert Bjork, John Dunlosky, & Nate Kornell, "Self-Regulated Learning: Beliefs, Techniques, and Illusions," *Annual Review of Psychology* 64 (2013): 417–44; Elizabeth Bjork and Robert Bjork, "Making Things Hard on Yourself, but in a Good Way: Creating Desirable Difficulties to Enhance Learning," in *Psychology and the Real World: Essays Illustrating Fundamental Contributions to Society*, eds. Morton A. Gernsbacher et al. (New York: Worth Publishers, 2011), 56–64; Robert Bjork, "Structuring the Conditions of Training to Achieve Elite Performance: Reflections on Elite Training Programs and Related Themes," in *Development of Professional Expertise: Toward Measurement of Expert Performance and Design of Optimal Learning Environments*, ed. K. A. Ericsson (New York: Cambridge University Press, 2009), 312–29; Robert Duke, Amy Simmons, and Carla Cash, "It's Not How Much; It's How," *Journal of Research in Music Education* 56 (January 2009): 310–321.

25. Alvaro Pascual-Leone et al., "The Plastic Human Brain Cortex," *Annual Reviews of Neuroscience* 28 (2005): 377–401.

26. Eleanor A. Maguire, Katherine Woollett, and Hugo J. Spiers, "London Taxi Drivers and Bus Drivers: A Structural MRI and Neuropsychological Analysis," *Hippocampus* 16 (2006): 1091–1101.

27. Michael Merzenich and Christophe deCharms, "Neural Representations, Experience, and Change," in *The Mind-Brain Continuum*, eds. Rodolfo R. Llinas and Patricia Smith Churchland (Cambridge, MA: MIT Press, 1996), 61–82; Gregg H. Recanzone, Christopher E. Schreiner, and Michael M. Merzenich, "Plasticity in the Frequency Representation of Primary Auditory Cortex Following Discrimination Training in Adult Owl Monkeys," *Journal of Neuroscience* 13 (1993): 87–103; Sharon Begley, *Train Your Mind, Change Your Brain* (New York: Ballantine Books, 2007).

28. K. Anders Ericsson, Michael J. Prietula, and Edward T. Cokely, "The Making of an Expert," *Harvard Business Review*, July 2007, http://hbr.org/2007/07/the-making-of-an-expert/ar/1.

29. Ibid.

30. Sean Gregory, "Practice, Made Perfect?" *Time*, April 15, 2013, http://content. time.com/time/magazine/article/0,9171,2140225,00.html. For more on Dan McLaughlin's journey, see his website: http://thedanplan.com/a-summary-of-the-dan-plan/.

31. Benjamin C. Storm, Robert A. Bjork, and Jennifer C. Storm, "Optimizing Retrieval as a Learning Event: When and Why Expanding Retrieval Practice Enhances Long-Term Retention," Memory & Cognition 38(2010): 244–53; Nate Kornell et al., "Spacing as the Friend of Both Memory and Induction in Younger and Older Adults," *Psychology and Aging* 25(2010): 498–503; Thomas Landauer and Robert Bjork, "Optimum Rehearsal Patterns and Name Learning," in *Practical Aspects of Memory, eds.* M. M. Gruneberg, P. E. Morris, and R. N. Sykes (New York: Academic Press, 1978), 625–32.

32. Steven Smith and Edward Vela, "Environmental Context-Dependent Memory: A Review and Meta-analysis," *Psychonomic Bulletin and Review* 8, no. 2 (2001): 203–20; *Steven Smith*, Arthur *Glenberg*, and Robert *Bjork*, "Environmental Context and Human Memory," *Memory & Cognition* 6 (1978), 342–53; Robert Kerr and Bernard Booth, "Specific and Varied Practice of Motor Skill," *Perceptual and Motor Skills* 46, no. 2 (1978): 395–401.

33. Monica Birnbaum et al., "Why Interleaving Enhances Inductive Learning: The Roles of Discrimination and Retrieval," *Memory & Cognition* 41(2013): 393–402; Doug Rohrer and Kelli Taylor, "The Shuffling of Mathematics Practice Problems Improves Learning," *Instructional Science* 35(2007), 481–98.

34. Nate Kornell and Robert Bjork, "Learning Concepts and Categories: Is Spacing the 'Enemy of Induction'?" *Psychological Science* 19 (2008): 585–592.

35. Bennett Schwartz et al., "Four Principles of Memory Improvement: A Guide to Improving Learning Efficiency," *International Journal of Creativity and Problem Solving* 21, no. 1 (2011): 7–15.

36. Robert Bjork, "Retrieval Practice and the Maintenance of Knowledge," in *Practical Aspects of Memory, Volume 2: Clinical and Educational Implications*, eds. M. M. Gruneberg, P. E. Morris, and R. N. Sykes (Hoboken: John Wiley & Sons, 1988), 396–401.

37. Nate Kornell, Matthew Hays, and Robert Bjork, "Unsuccessful Retrieval Attempts Enhance Subsequent Learning," *Journal of Experimental Psychology: Learning, Memory, and Cognition* 35, no. 4 (2009): 989–98; Henry Roediger and Jeffrey Karpicke, "Test-Enhanced Learning: Taking Memory Tests Improves Long-Term Retention," *Psychological Science* 17, no. 3 (2006): 249–255; Robert Bjork, "Retrieval as a Memory Modifier," in *Information Processing and Cognition: The Loyola Symposium*, ed. R. Solso (Hillsdale, NJ:

Lawrence Erlbaum Associates, 1975), 123–144; Bjork and Bjork, "Making Things Hard on Yourself."

38. Bjork, "Structuring the Conditions of Training"; Richard Schmidt and Robert Bjork, "New Conceptualizations of Practice: Common Principles in Three Paradigms Suggest New Concepts for Training," *Psychological Science*, 3 no. 4 (1992): 207–17.

39. George Kohlrieser, Susan Goldsworthy, and Duncan Coombe, *Care to Dare: Unleashing Astonishing Potential through Secure Base Leadership* (San Francisco: Jossey-Bass, 2012); John Bowlby, *A Secure Base: Parent-Child Attachment and Healthy Human Development* (New York: Basic Books, 1988); Amy Edmondson, "Strategies for Learning from Failure," *Harvard Business Review*, April 2011, http://hbr.org/2011/04/strategies-for-learning-from-failure/ar/1; Amy Edmondson, "The Competitive Imperative of Learning," *Harvard Business Review*, July 2008, http://hbr.org/2008/07/the-competitive-imperative-of-learning/ar/1.

40. U.S. Army, *Leader's Guide to After Action Reviews*, September 2011, http://www.jackson.army.mil/sites/leaderdevelopment/docs/710.

41. Taiichi Ohno, "Ask 'Why' Five Times about Every Matter," *Toyota Traditions*, March 2006, http://www.toyota-global.com/company/toyota_traditions/quality/mar_apr_2006.html.

42. Adapted from W. Chan Kim and Renee Mauborgne, "Blue Ocean Strategy: From Theory to Practice," *California Management Review* 47, no. 3 (Spring 2005).

43. Rubinstein and Firstenberg, *The Minding Organization*.

44. Rita Gunther McGrath, "Failing by Design," *Harvard Business Review*, April 2011, http://hbr.org/2011/04/failing-by-design/ar/1; Polly LaBarre, "Provoking the Future," *Harvard Business Review Blog Network*, July 20, 2011, http://blogs.hbr.org/2011/07/provoking-the-future/; Jim Lavoie, "The Innovation Engine at Rite-Solutions: Lessons from the CEO," *Journal of Prediction Markets* 3 (2009): 1–11; William Taylor, "Here's an Idea: Let Everyone Have Ideas," *New York Times*, March 26, 2006, http://www.nytimes.com/2006/03/26/business/yourmoney/26mgmt.html.

45. William Taylor, "Here's an Idea: Let Everyone Have Ideas," *New York Times*, March 26, 2006, http://www.nytimes.com/2006/03/26/business/yourmoney/26mgmt.html.

46. Peter Drucker, "The Discipline of Innovation," *Harvard Business Review*, November-December 1988.

47. Peter Drucker, *Innovation and Entrepreneurship* (New York: Harper Business, Reprint Edition, 2006).

48. Karen Dillon, "'I Think of My Failures as a Gift': An Interview with A.G. Lafley," *Harvard Business Review*, April 2011, http://hbr.org/2011/04/i-think-of-my-failures-as-a-gift/ar/1.

49. Matthew May, *The Elegant Solution: Toyota's Formula for Mastering Innovation* (New York: Free Press, 2006).

CHAPTER 7   SHAPE YOUR FUTURE

1. Aaron Wildavsky, *The Nursing Father: Moses as a Political Leader* (Tuscaloosa: University of Alabama Press, 1984).

About the Authors

Iris R. Firstenberg, PhD, holds a joint appointment at UCLA as an adjunct associate professor in the Department of Psychology and the Anderson School of Management. Since 2005, she has been teaching a hugely popular course for MBA students, titled "Thinking on Your Feet." Iris teaches seminars on leadership development and innovative thinking for many Fortune 500 organizations, and she is coauthor with Moshe of two prior books.

Moshe F. Rubinstein, PhD, is an internationally renowned authority on problem solving and creativity in organizations. He is a professor emeritus at the UCLA School of Engineering and Applied Science and advises many major corporations on innovation. He has won numerous teaching awards and has written ten books, which have been translated into several languages. In January 2000, Moshe was named one of the top 20 professors of the century at UCLA.

Index